S0-AAD-518

MAKE IT ACCURATE

MAKE IT ACCURATE
Get the Maximum Performance from Your Hunting Rifle

Craig T. Boddington

Safari Press Inc.

P.O. Box 3095, Long Beach, CA 90803-0095, USA

Make It Accurate copyright 1999 © by Craig T. Boddington. All rights reserved. No part of this publication may be used or reproduced in any form or by any means, electronic or mechanical reproduction, including photocopy, recording, or any information storage and retrieval system, without permission from the publisher.

The trademark Safari Press ® is registered with the U.S. Patent and Trademark Office and in other countries.

Boddington, Craig T.

Safari Press Inc.

1999, Long Beach, California

ISBN 1-57157-150-7

Library of Congress Catalog Card Number: 98-61282

10 9 8 7 6 5 4 3 2

Readers wishing to receive the Safari Press catalog, featuring many fine books on big-game hunting, wingshooting, and sporting firearms, should write to Safari Press Inc., P.O. Box 3095, Long Beach, CA 90803, USA. Tel: (714) 894-9080 or visit our Web site at www.safaripress.com.

TABLE OF CONTENTS

ACKNOWLEDGMENTS

Any writer has many people to thank when, after months and sometimes years of effort, a book finally reaches completion. I'm especially grateful to my wife, Bernadette, for her patience—not only during my all too frequent absences but also when I'm present. Under normal circumstances I'm no piece of cake to be around, but that's especially true when I'm in the middle of a book project! The same thanks goes to the rest of my family, and especially to my parents—the two totally objective fans on whom I can always count. Of course, my longtime publisher, Ludo Wurfbain and his wife, Jacque, deserve much credit. Ludo is a far better "idea guy" than I am, and whenever I get stuck his judgment is always sound. Every writer needs a good editor, and I'm also grateful to Ludo, Jacque, and crew for cleaning up my messes.

I suppose that the process of writing differs little from one subject to another, but what I know about is writing about guns and hunting. A hunting book is a relatively simple matter of recounting experiences, but it strikes me that when embarking on a more or less technical project such as this, a non-technical klutz such as myself is operating pretty much in a vacuum. I'm therefore especially grateful to my many friends in the industry who knowingly and unknowingly contributed their knowledge to this volume. This list is long and not inclusive, but it must include great gunmakers such as Mark Bansner, Jim Brockman, Mel Forbes, Kenny Jarrett, John Lazzeroni, David Miller, Kerry O'Day, Rich Reiley, and Lex Webernick; bullet and ammunition manufacturers such as Larry Barnett, Randy Brooks, Jack Carter, Chub Eastman, Steve Hornady, Mike Jordan, Bob Nosler, Lee Reid, and Sam Sanjabi; and optics guys like Jim Morey, Terry Moore, and Gary Williams. And a special thanks to my buddy Geoff Miller of Rogue River Rifleworks/John Rigby & Co. Geoff is one of the most astute riflemen I know, and he was generous with both his time and talents throughout this project. Moreover, the concept of this book was altogether his brainchild, so I'm doubly grateful.

DEDICATION

This one's for Bernadette.

CHAPTER ONE

THE HUNTING RIFLE

In my day I have been a passable shotgunner, both in competition and in the field. I own a number of shotguns, and a couple of them are pretty good guns. But if the wingshooters and trapshooters and skeet shooters and all the rest will forgive me, even the good shotguns that I own are relatively simple tools in my mind. I haven't competed with a handgun for more than twenty years, but to this day I'm not ashamed of my handgunning ability. I own a few handguns, and a couple of them, too, are pretty good guns. I hope the serious pistoleros, too, will forgive me, for in my eyes handguns are also relatively simple tools. I'm first and foremost a rifleman.

As you might imagine, I own a number of rifles. As with handguns, I haven't competed in any rifle events for twenty years or more. Every rifle I own is a hunting rifle. Now *that's* something special! To be perfectly honest, my rifles, too, are actually fairly simple tools. Each is a mating of stock, action, and rifled barrel, and each wears some type of sight to steer the bullet along its way. The sum of any of them is just a couple of dozen parts. None of them approach the complexity of a lawnmower engine, and all of them—in principle if not in detail—are based on designs at least a century old. They're special because I'm a hunter, and they are *hunting rifles*.

There are quite a few of them. Some are old friends, and some are recent acquaintances. A lot of different types of hunting are represented among them. There are small-game rifles, varmint rifles, deer rifles, rifles for larger game. There are dangerous-game rifles, and there are long-range rifles. Some have open sights, some have scopes, and some have both. There are a number of calibers represented, and there are even some duplicates. A very few were skillfully crafted by a custom maker and are stocked in the finest walnut. A few others were crafted just as skillfully but wear fiberglass. Many came right out of a factory box. Some are very specialized in purpose, and some are very versatile.

You see, a hunting rifle can take many forms. It can be chambered to a myriad of cartridges. It can have any of several stock styles, and its dimensions can be whatever suits its owner. Any of the known action types can be used . . . and perhaps some that are not yet known. It can be sighted in any manner its owner chooses, and it can be lovingly cared for or it can be abused.

It is not my purpose herein to tell you what your hunting rifle should look like, or how it should be sighted or stocked or chambered. Of course I have my preferences, and where it's appropriate I'll give them to you—but your preferences needn't be mine. You are under no obligation to follow them in order to receive your value for these pages, for such recommendations are not the purpose of this book. Instead, my purpose here is to help you choose a rifle that will best suit your needs . . . and then help you get the best performance from your choice.

You see, a hunting rifle can take many forms. I don't know what kind of hunting you pursue. It is possible that there is such a thing as that elusive "all-round rifle" that my gunwriting colleagues and I have spilled so much ink in pursuit of, but I have never seen one. I have seen some very versatile rifles, and I even own several of them. I have also seen a lot of very specialized rifles, and I own several of them as well. Let's say that you, Reader A, are an eastern whitetail hunter who spends most of your hunting hours in a treestand. Now let's say that you, Reader B, are also a whitetail hunter, but you hunt your whitetails on the Great Plains. Chances are we can think of a whole lot of rifles that would work very well for both of you . . . most of the time. The "perfect" rifle for each of you, however, is probably quite different.

The trick is to choose the rifle that in action, caliber, and stock design is best suited to your hunting needs. Even so, that perfect rifle could probably take a number of different forms and certainly could be chambered to a variety of calibers. What is most important is that *you* believe it's the best choice for your purposes, for you must be steadfast in that belief in order to have the confidence you need to allow your rifle to do its best work.

Whether a fine custom piece or a straightforward factory rifle, your choice is *your* hunting rifle. And whatever form it takes, in order to deserve that title it must share several characteristics with all other hunting rifles. It must first and foremost be absolutely, completely, totally reliable. It has to function properly each and every time you cycle the action and

Hunting rifles cannot be classed by action type any more than caliber. Depending on the chambering and configuration, a bolt-action, single-shot, or lever action—or, for that matter, a slide action or semiautomatic—could be suitable for virtually any type of hunting.

The hunting rifle is a most special firearm, carried to special places. Whatever your hunting rifle looks like, and whatever caliber it's chambered to, it's essential that it fit you, and that you like it. Only then can you have the confidence in it that you must have.

squeeze the trigger. It cannot occasionally fail to feed, extract, or eject; its safety must be reliable.

It does not necessarily have to possess tack-driving accuracy. Different types of hunting have different requirements. A rifle intended for varmint hunting must be more accurate than a rifle intended for deer hunting in close cover. A rifle intended for hunting Cape buffalo need not be as accurate as a rifle intended for hunting pronghorns at long range. However, this is absolute: It must be accurate enough for the hunting you intend to do with it. Of equal importance, and equally absolute, it must be consistent in its accuracy. Yes, there may be hiccups. A hard knock on a mountain can shift any scope, and an unexpected downpour can cause wood to swell. But barring exceptional circumstances, day to day, week to week, year to year, a hunting rifle should put its bullets in the same place and deliver whatever level of accuracy it is capable of.

Hunting rifles can be long or short, light or heavy, and can have a variety of actions, stock styles and materials, finishes, and chamberings. The trick is to match the rifle as closely as possible to your needs.

There is one more characteristic that a true hunting rifle must possess. It must fit its owner. It must come to the shoulder smoothly and on target. It has to feel like an extension of your eyes, arms, and hands, for indeed that is exactly what a hunting rifle is.

These sound like very stringent and severe requirements. Indeed they are, but none requires that you invest in a custom rifle. And, by the same token, spending thousands of dollars on a custom rifle does not necessarily fill all of these requirements! There are very sound reasons for going the custom route, but it is not essential to do so to achieve the reliability, accuracy, and handling qualities required of a hunting rifle. As these pages progress, I will make suggestions on the sensible selection of a suitable rifle—but keep in mind that I don't have all the answers. I have at least a passing familiarity with most North American

The .30-06 is one of my all-time favorite cartridges, and one of the most versatile and useful. It isn't out of place anywhere in North America, from eastern whitetails all the way to Alaska.

hunting situations, but I don't claim to be an expert on anyone's home turf. *You* must ultimately decide what's best for you—and so long as your choice gives you the confidence you need to be successful, I would never argue with it.

There are no absolutes, very few wrong answers, and many right ones. I will cover some of the basic choices and characteristics that should be taken into consideration. Then we will proceed to the various steps that should be taken to properly set up your hunting rifle for the field—and also a few steps that you may wish to take to enhance your rifle's performance. Since it would be totally impossible to go through the various steps of mounting a scope, checking bedding, and working up loads for all—or even a small fraction—of the various choices available in hunting rifles, I will take two very similar rifles through these steps.

In doing so, I have definitely made a conscious choice that may or may not be ideally suited to your hunting, and which you may or may not wish to follow. Both of the rifles are bolt-action Remington Model 700s, and both are chambered to .30-06. One is a well-used but not abused, wooden-stocked Model 700 ADL. The other is a brand-new Model 700 ADL, synthetic-stocked. The former was purchased off the used-gun rack at our local gunshop; the latter was ordered direct from Remington.

As we will see in succeeding chapters, I chose the .30-06 because it is one of the most versatile of our cartridges, and offers one of the widest selections in factory loads—as well as the widest selection of component bullets and a ninety-year history of available reloading data. I chose the bolt-action because of its simplicity, reliability, and tendency toward accuracy. I did not choose the Model 700 because I think it is necessarily the best. It is the bolt action that I am most familiar with, and it has a well-deserved reputation for accuracy. I should say right now, however, that the same experiments could be conducted equally well with a Winchester Model 70, Browning A-Bolt, Weatherby Mark V, Savage 110, or any of several dozen other bolt actions.

Although the two rifles are basically identical, I thought it would be interesting to work with one in wood and one in synthetic. It probably will be interesting; as I write these lines I have not yet fired either rifle or even mounted scopes. So we'll all learn as we go, and we'll see what happens.

It's probably needless to say, but I should point out up front that all rifles are individuals, and that both of these Model 700s are individual rifles. We will take both through the various steps of scope mounting, checking and perhaps revamping the bedding, and finding what ammo—both factory and handload—each likes the best. What is most important are the processes. I seriously doubt that each of these rifles will deliver the same level of accuracy, or that each will perform optimally with the same loads. I doubt even more seriously that your rifle, whatever you choose, will respond in exactly the same way. So don't expect to follow this book like a formula. Rifles are almost as individualistic as strong-willed humans, and each has different likes and dislikes. Instead, pay attention to the thought processes and procedures as we set up these two almost identical—but unique—rifles for hunting.

Once the scopes are selected and mounted, the mechanics and the bedding are found satisfactory, and the rifles have told us

These are the two "project rifles" selected for this book, a new Remington Model 700 ADL in synthetic stock, and a used Model 700 ADL in wooden stock. Both are chambered to .30-06. At this time they are not yet hunting rifles . . . but we'll hope to fix that as the book progresses.

what loads they like best, we'll turn to the little things that will enhance your rifle's performance in the field—slings, scope covers, rests, devices to reduce recoil, and such. We'll work our way through sighting in for hunting, and we'll also discuss gun care. This last is important for several reasons. We expect a lot from our hunting rifles, and well we should. When we've sat in the cold for enough days, climbed enough hills, glassed enough game, and finally worked our way close enough for a shot at our chosen animal, we expect our rifles to perform. We expect them to fire and to deliver their bullets in accordance with our aim.

A hunting rifle is a simple tool but a very loyal one. It can deliver this performance through a lifetime of hard use—and can deliver the same performance to our children and grandchildren. All it asks in return for such faithful performance is a modest amount of care, both to ensure its accuracy and to enhance its longevity.

The two rifles I have chosen to work through these various steps may not yet deserve the title of "hunting rifle," but by the time we're finished I'm sure they will. Mind you, they will not be *my* hunting rifles. I'm totally left-handed, and to avoid confusion in the photography both of our project Model 700s are right-handed rifles. So, as I write these lines I can't help but think of *my* hunting rifles. None in my gun safes go back to my earliest hunting days; I lost all of those in a burglary in 1981. I still mourn their loss, but some of the rifles I have today have been with me over many tough miles. All have taken game for me. I use some more than others, but I own no rifles that have not been hunting with me.

Some shoot better than others, but all shoot well enough for their intended purposes, and each and every one gives me pleasure to heft—all bring back fond memories, and each reminds me of a place I should take it in some season to come. Since this book is about selecting and setting up *your* hunting rifle, it's only fair that you should ask about my favorite rifle. With apologies, there is no easy answer . . . and perhaps no answer at all. I do have two left-handed .30-06 rifles in Remington Model 700 actions, one in wood and one in synthetic. The former is from the Remington Custom Shop, the latter by Kenny Jarrett. Both shoot better than I can, and I would consider them the most versatile of my battery. But I don't love them more than my David Miller 7mm Remington Magnum, a wonderful execution of fine wood and metal and also a very versatile rifle. I'm also exceptionally fond of a Mark Bansner 7x57, and a Dakota .270, and a Match Grade Arms .300 Winchester Magnum. I could pick up any one of these rifles and be perfectly well-armed for at least ninety percent of my hunting. But to say that any of these is my favorite would mean excluding the lever actions—Winchesters in Models 88, 94, and 71—and each has its place in both my heart and my hunting. It would also mean excluding my varmint rifles and my .22s, and my long-range rig, the Rogue River 8mm Remington Magnum. It would also mean ignoring my badly battered left-hand-converted Model 70 in .375, and my new but much-prized .416 Rigby. And then I must think about my absent comrades: my long gone Bishop-stocked .264 that took so much of my first game, stolen in 1981; two equally long gone double .470s, one stolen and one sold; and of course there were others.

As I think about it, I simply cannot tell you which is my favorite rifle, or which is my favorite caliber. Some of my rifles are very specialized, and some serve a variety of purposes—but each is a hunting rifle in every sense, and each carries the memories of hunts past and the anticipation of hunts to come. And, after all, it doesn't really matter which is *my* favorite hunting rifle. What's important is that *your* hunting rifle be well suited to your needs, and that it delivers to you the best performance it is capable of. So let's forge ahead in the selection of *your* hunting rifle. Whatever your choice or choices happen to be, I hope your rifles give you as much enjoyment as I receive from mine.

═══ CHAPTER TWO ═══

SPECIAL PURPOSE OR ALL-ROUND?

Perhaps the most basic decision in selecting a hunting rifle is determining exactly what kind of rifle you need. Obviously this should be based primarily on the kind of hunting you do—or wish to do in the future. To some extent, too, your choice should probably take into account the rifles you already own. Is your new rifle to be a replacement for an old friend? Will you use it for the hunting you normally do, or for something you're planning? Do you wish it to offer greater capability than your current rifles, or is it intended for different purposes altogether?

Because there are so many different kinds of hunting rifles, in this discussion we will concentrate primarily on rifles for hunting big game, excluding the varmint rifles and .22 rimfires. However, even though very little specific reference will be made to these types of rifles, much of this book can be applied equally well to small-game rifles and varminters. We can simplify the discussion somewhat by limiting ourselves to big-game rifles, but even that is a very broad subject. There is a tremendous spectrum of big game and big-game hunting, and a tremendous diversity of rifles intended for the purpose.

Although I have probably used—and abused—the term just as much as any gunwriter, I don't think there is truly any such thing as an "all-round rifle." Even if we exclude small game and varmints, the universe of big-game hunting remains so large that it is ridiculous to seriously believe one rifle can be well suited to all. A rifle that is ideal for white-tailed deer is unlikely to be ideal for Alaskan brown bear, and even less likely to be ideal for Cape buffalo and elephant. For that matter, a whitetail rifle perfectly suited for the southern swamps and eastern forests is unlikely to be equally perfect for Great Plains whitetails, and even less likely to be well suited for hunting Coues whitetails in the Southwestern mountains. So I can't embrace the premise of one rifle for everything.

There are, however, a great many extremely versatile rifles that will cover a wide range of hunting purposes. There are also specialized rifles that are perfect for just a few applications. It could well be that your needs are best suited by a very specialized type of rifle, but you must understand their limitations as well as their capabilities. In our thinking we often tend to classify rifles by caliber alone. This is pretty easy to do. A dangerous-game

Whatever rifle you choose, you must take into account the kind of hunting you have in mind. A special-purpose rig may be perfect, or you may be better served by a more versatile rifle. There is relatively little hunting in the world that I can't do with my David Miller 7mm Remington Magnum.

rifle, for instance, can readily be identified as being chambered to the .375 H&H, or something more powerful. A long-range rifle will almost certainly be chambered to a cartridge that is modest in caliber, long on powder capacity, and very fast. This is an oversimplification. Specialized rifles can take many forms, and there is usually much more to their configuration than caliber alone. A .375 H&H, for instance, isn't automatically the perfect brown bear rifle. Sighting equipment, barrel length, and type of action are also important.

In this "age of specialization" that we seem to be living in, it might be possible to develop "the perfect rifle" for each and every type of game and local hunting condition. That isn't up to me. It's up to you to decide what constitutes the perfect rifle for your type of hunting. Sometimes your choices will also, by happy coincidence, be fairly versatile. In other cases your idea of the

This is the famed Beanfield Rifle by Kenny Jarrett. Long in the barrel, chambered to fast, flat cartridges, and relatively heavy, this is a classic example of a long-range rifle . . . and above all, it has the accuracy to be worthy of the title. This rifle, chambered to .300 Jarrett, averages one-third-inch groups.

This is David Miller's 1998 Chihuahua Coues deer, dropped cleanly at more than 500 yards after five hours of stalking and waiting. This is easier said than done; Miller has spent years and thousands upon thousands of rounds honing his shooting skills.

perfect rifle may be limited in its versatility. If so, you must then decide whether you really want a rifle quite that specialized, or if you would prefer something not quite so perfect for much of your hunting but better suited to a wider range of use.

Specialized rifles can take many forms, so many that it would be impossible to attempt to cover them all. Some common varieties that often arise in discussion are: long-range rifles, dangerous-game rifles, ultra-lightweight rifles, and close-cover rifles. Let's take a look at the configuration, capabilities, and limitations of these classes of hunting rifles, and then we'll look at some more versatile options.

LONG-RANGE RIFLES

The long-range rifle has become sort of a "fad" among American hunters today. Although there have long been at least a few hunters interested in expanding the range envelope, the current trend can be attributed largely to South Carolina gunmaker Kenny Jarrett's famed "Beanfield Rifle." Jarrett is a gunmaker, a benchrest shooter, and a lifelong whitetail hunter. During his hunting career he has seen the white-tailed deer expand its populations from the southern swamps into the farm country. He reasoned that a hunting rifle that shot flat and fast and embodied near-benchrest accuracy would enable him—and his customers—to reach out across those southern soybean fields and bag bucks that were simply out of sensible range of conventional hunting rifles.

Jarrett's rifles got a lot of publicity, and over the last decade or so a great many good custom makers—and many of the factories—have joined him in offering "long-range rifles." Obviously they aren't just for southern whitetail hunters. Many whitetail hunters in the Great Plains and the Canadian prairies have gravitated to such rifles. So have some sheep hunters, mule

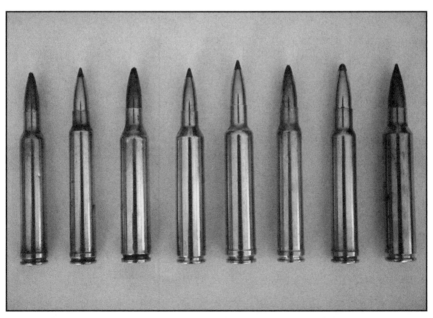

Left to right: .300 Weatherby Magnum, .300 Jarrett, .300 Pegasus (A-Square), 7.82 Warbird (Lazzeroni), .30-.378 Weatherby, 8mm Remington Magnum, .340 Weatherby Magnum, 8.59 Titan (Lazzeroni). There are relatively few serious long-range cartridges, but cartridge alone doesn't define the long-range rifle. Accuracy is far more important than speed.

deer hunters, Coues whitetail hunters, and even elk hunters. Some, in fact, use this type of rifle for virtually all of their hunting . . . but this does not imply that a long-range rifle is for everybody.

In configuration, most serious long-range rifles are bolt-actions, this because the turnbolt is the action most likely to deliver the desired degree of accuracy. The barrel is generally fairly long, almost never less than 26 inches and often 28 inches or more. This is desirable to wring the maximum velocity out of the cartridge. The barrels are usually fairly stiff as well. A stiff barrel is not inherently more accurate than a thin barrel, but it is easier to make a heavy barrel shoot consistently well. The stock is most likely to be synthetic or laminate, but it can be well-bedded wood. It will often be of generous proportion, wide and deep in the butt to dampen recoil. The scope will most likely be a powerful variable, with a maximum magnification from about 12X to as much as 20X. The rifle will probably be fairly heavy, a combination of heavy barrel, big stock, and heavy scope. The weight not only makes the rifle as stable as possible but also dampens recoil and helps the rifle to be "shootable." Its cartridge will be fast and flat-shooting, but the caliber depends on the game to be hunted. The general range is from .25 (for small deer and pronghorn) to .33 for elk.

This is what the long-range rifle *looks* like. But just as not all rifles have what it takes to be called hunting rifles, not all rifles that look like this are truly long-range rifles. The most essential characteristic of the long-range rifle is that it be very, very accurate. Whether it comes from a major manufacturer or the best custom maker, a long-range rifle should, with the right ammo and a competent shooter, deliver groups of not more than half an inch at 100 yards. Tighter groups are better yet. Factory rifles, perhaps with a bit of help in the bedding and *very* careful ammo selection, can deliver this level of accuracy. Many top custom makers can routinely deliver it as well. But keep in mind that looks aren't everything in this game—the rifle must walk the walk as well as talk the talk.

The long-range rifle must, quite simply, allow shooting with confidence and deadly effect at exceptionally long distances. It is not my purpose here to define long range, or to explore the ethics of long-range shooting. Most versatile hunting rifles chambered to flat-shooting cartridges are fully capable, in the right hands, of enabling good hits to at least 400 yards. That's a very long distance, and it's in the neighborhood of the 400-yard mark that the *real* long-range rifles come into their own. Although there are limits out there somewhere, how much beyond that distance the range can be stretched depends on the shooter's ability, the cartridge, and the size of the game.

The requirement of the shooter's ability is obvious. When I talk about the cartridge, I do not mean its trajectory. A very flat trajectory helps but is not essential. By the time you get to 400 yards you must *know* your cartridge's trajectory, and so long as you know it, a few inches more or less of drop are not important.

This is my Rogue River 8mm Remington Magnum with a beautiful urial sheep I shot in far-off Turkmenistan. You must have faith in the rifle and genuine expectations of a long shot to drag a true long-range rifle up a sheep mountain!

The cartridge is important because it must deliver enough energy to ensure a clean kill. Size of the game is important not in terms of offering a bigger target but rather for a reason similar to the cartridge's importance: The larger the game, the more energy you must deliver at the animal. Thus a cartridge that is theoretically adequate for deer at 600 yards may not necessarily be adequate for elk at 600 yards.

I think I can best explain the capability of the long-range rifle with a few words about the exploits of Tucson gunmaker David Miller. Miller is a great custom gunmaker and a fine rifle shot. He's also obsessed with the little Coues whitetail of his southwestern mountains. Up until about a decade ago Miller had taken many nice Coues whitetails but never a huge buck. Although he has always been an unusually good marksman, he was doing his hunting with conventional sporters. Like most of us, the range at which he could make shots with confidence was limited to about 400 yards and change.

Miller wanted to take bigger Coues whitetails. Glassing with big optics, he had seen a number of big bucks that he just couldn't get close to. He reasoned that if he could just reach out a bit farther, his chances would improve. So he started working on his long-range shooting, and developing his concept of the ideal long-range rifle. The rifle evolved into the laminate-stocked David Miller Marksman—fairly heavy, very accurate, extremely stable. Miller's own Marksmen, an identical pair, are both chambered to .300 Weatherby Magnum and wear Leupold 6.5-20X scopes. In the last decade, using these rifles, Miller has entered an astonishing six Coues whitetails into the Boone and Crockett Club's *Records of North American Big Game*.

The closest shot on those six bucks was about 450 yards. I will not quote the distance of the longest shot. Just three days ago, as I write this, Miller and I glassed an old, heavy-horned buck far up on a little round butte in the mountains of Chihuahua, Mexico. There was absolutely no way to approach this buck for a close shot. Miller climbed off our mountain and worked his way up into some rimrock across from the little butte. It took him two hours to get into position, and by then the buck was bedded. Miller waited three more hours until the buck got up, and then he shot him at a distance of 550 yards. That is the capability of the long-range rifle.

The limitations lie partly with the rifle and partly with the shooter. The long-range rifle is heavy, and it will become burdensome on foot hunts in rough country. The aficionados of this rifle put up gladly with the extra weight. I've carried my heavy, long-barreled Rogue River 8mm Remington Magnum up many a mountain—but I've often questioned my own sanity in doing so. The long-range rifle can be made to handle well, but in close quarters a long barrel isn't necessarily the best choice. A very big scope, too, can be a detriment if a close shot is called for. You don't carry such a rifle for the *occasional* long shot but rather because your hunting is most likely to yield an opportunity at some distance.

A dangerous game rifle must be adequate in caliber, but that's really just the beginning. While accuracy is of primary importance in a long-range rifle, reliability and handling qualities are the hallmarks of the dangerous-game rifle. This is my beatup old pre-'64 Model 70 in .375 H&H.

The real limitation, however, lies with the shooter. The long-range rifle is heavier and more cumbersome than may be optimum, and in fast-breaking situations is probably not as fast or responsive as a more conventional hunting rifle—but it will do. The main limitation is that very few of us have the skill, discipline, and patience to utilize such a rifle's capability. Just purchasing a long-range rifle does not make you a long-range shooter. Before you attempt shooting at extreme range, you must *know* your rifle's trajectory. You must *know* the range. You must *know* how to read the wind and the uphill/downhill angle. With skill and practice, long-range shooting is not unethical, but to attempt a shot at game without this knowledge is irresponsible.

Such knowledge comes only from long and exhaustive practice. Tight 100-yard groups are only the start; the long-range shooter must actually shoot a great deal at extreme ranges. It is also almost mandatory to invest significant time in the care and feeding of your rifle. It is extremely unlikely that factory ammunition will deliver the accuracy you must have. David Miller, for instance, uses an ultrasound wave comparator to sort not only his cases but also his bullets to ensure absolute uniformity.

Miller is obviously a very intense guy . . . but he is successfully shooting the smallest of big game at the longest of distances! For larger game and shorter ranges, the requirements may not be quite so severe, but the most important thing to remember about long-range rifles is that they are a waste of your time and money unless you are willing to make a serious commitment to their use, care, and feeding.

DANGEROUS-GAME RIFLES

The most obvious thing about a rifle for dangerous game is that it is powerful and large of caliber. By "dangerous game" I'm speaking of *really* dangerous. A black bear can be dangerous, and so can a wild hog—but here we're talking about our largest bears, African lion, and thick-skinned game such as Cape buffalo and elephant. Even so, caliber is not the only definition. I'd be

In rough country, especially on a backpack hunt, gun weight makes a big difference. It can even make the difference between getting to the game and not getting to the game. This is my Match Grade Arms .300 Winchester Magnum, weighing in at about six pounds.

perfectly happy with a well-appointed .338 for grizzly, but in today's Africa I'd be nervous about a .375 for elephant. So let's ignore caliber except to say that it must be big enough to get the job done. Instead, let's talk about what a dangerous-game rifle should *look* like.

Many could argue the point, but for me it must hold more than one shot. In some contexts it could be a heavy double, but the primary action for housing this kind of power is the bolt-action. The bolt-action will house the largest of cartridges, and it has the reliability to function despite dust, sand, rain, and freezing cold. The rifle will probably have a medium to short barrel—rarely more than 24 inches—and although it may be built heavy to dampen recoil, it must handle responsively and come up almost like a shotgun.

It may be open-sighted, it may be scoped, or it may carry both systems—but whatever sight is chosen must be absolutely goof-proof and exceptionally rugged. Moreover, the sights on a

The action on the Match Grade Arms rifle has been skeletonized, the stock is light, and the barrel is very slim. And yet this rifle shoots extremely tight groups, proof positive that light barrels can shoot as well as heavy barrels if the gun is made right.

dangerous-game rifle must address the very real potential of stopping a charge at close range. A low-range variable or low-power scope may be chosen, and this will give the dangerous-game rifle a level of versatility—but not enough for the rifle to be well suited for shots much beyond 200 yards.

Big-bore rifles are often very accurate, but the dangerous-game rifle does not really need a high level of accuracy. An open-sighted double rifle, for instance, that groups both barrels within 4 inches at 100 yards is perfectly adequate for use on dangerous game. Far more important than raw accuracy are handling qualities and absolute reliability. The dangerous-game rifle *must* have the accuracy and the sighting equipment to enable precise shot placement at sensible dangerous-game ranges—rarely more than 100 yards. The primary capability, however, is the ability to stop a charge when the chips are down.

Most such rifles of very large caliber are extremely limited in their application. Scoped dangerous-game rifles in .375 and even .416 have the capability for shooting out to 250 yards or so but are certainly not the best tools for such work. Gun weight, unnecessary recoil, and practical range restrictions are all severe limitations of the dangerous-game rifle in most hunting applications.

ULTRA-LIGHTWEIGHT RIFLES

Another trend in American hunting rifles is the desire for very light weight. Mel Forbes's Ultralight Arms is a classic example; Mel can make a bolt-action sporter that weighs less than five pounds, and he can make them shoot. Other custom and semi-custom makers specialize in this arena, and many of the major manufacturers have lightweight models as well: Winchester's Featherweight, Remington's Mountain Rifle, Ruger's Ultralight.

The general conception is that a lightweight rifle will have a synthetic stock. This is most often the case, but it doesn't have to be. Depending on its construction, synthetic isn't necessarily lighter than wood, and wooden-stocked rifles can be made very light.

What a light rifle is, regardless of its construction, is *light*. Obviously there are varying degrees. A "normal" bolt-action sporter, unscoped, will usually weigh somewhere between 7 and $7^3/_4$ pounds. Most synthetic-stocked rifles lean toward the former weight; most walnut-stocked sporters are closer to the latter weight. To get that weight down you must remove material, pure and simple. Lightweights tend to have shorter, more slender barrels and slender stocks. The stocks must be selectively hollowed out, if wood. If synthetic, they will probably be a foam-filled shell.

To get the weight down even more, the action must be trimmed down as well. A short action reduces weight, and the action can be selectively "skeletonized" as well. Wherever possible, alloys lighter than steel can be employed, such as in the floorplate and trigger-guard assembly. Most lightweights are bolt-actions, but a single-shot can be built exceedingly light as well.

Now, once you have a very light rifle you must be careful not to add unnecessary weight in scope and mounts, else you're defeating the purpose. Two-piece bases save a couple of ounces, and a compact scope of modest power saves a few more.

The lightweight rifle's major claim to fame is simply that it's a pleasure to carry over rough or steep terrain. Given sensible construction, the lightweight rifle is not less rugged than a full-size model. It is also not inherently less accurate. A pencil-thin barrel does not in itself shoot less well than a sporter-weight barrel or even a bull barrel. The difference is that it is harder to bed a thin barrel so that it will shoot well, and a thin barrel will heat up quicker. This means that a light-barreled rifle may shoot

The old Winchester Model 71 in .348 Winchester remains one of my favorite hunting rifles, but its range is limited. That's OK so long as it's used in country suited to the rifle's capabilities.

The old .30-30 Winchester is a very effective deer cartridge, partly because of the rapid energy transfer of its flatpoint bullets. Carbines are often chambered for this cartridge. These carbines make very fine deer guns, provided the country doesn't require shots much past 150 yards or so.

tight three-shot groups but is less likely to shoot tight five-shot groups than a rifle with a heavier barrel. This is insignificant in most hunting situations.

So why wouldn't everyone want a very light rifle? Several reasons. First, since a slender barrel is more finicky in its bedding than a heavy barrel, it's usually (not always!) more finicky about the loads that it shoots well. Second, in some applications you may want a larger scope than is sensible to mount on a very light rifle. Third, recoil is a function of gun weight as well as caliber. Later on we'll discuss muzzle brakes and such, but the simple fact is that light rifles have more felt recoil than heavier rifles of like caliber—and the easiest way to reduce recoil is to add gun weight. So if you want a very light rifle that is manageable in recoil, you pretty much need to limit its power. Fourth, while light rifles are a pleasure to carry, it's also a fact that heavier rifles are more stable and easier to shoot well—especially when you're excited and out of breath.

None of this is meant to imply that light rifles are bad. On a sheep mountain a 6-pound rifle is wonderful to carry—but an 8-pound rifle is easier to shoot, kicks less, and will probably deliver similar accuracy with a greater variety of ammo.

CLOSE-COVER RIFLES

A dangerous-game rifle is also a rifle intended for use at close quarters, but here we're talking about the so-called "brush rifle." It may be intended for black bear, or it may be intended for hunting deer or even elk in very thick cover. It doesn't have to be light in weight; a lot of close-cover hunting is done from stands. It does have to be very fast, and it will probably chamber a cartridge that is large in caliber, fires a heavy bullet, and is relatively low in velocity. In essence, the close-cover rifle is a short-range affair, designed to deliver a heavy blow and to handle very quickly.

Any action type can be used, but the most typical close-cover rifle is probably a lever-action chambered to one of the so-called "brush cartridges"—.35 Remington, .375 Winchester, .444 Marlin, .45-70. This is somewhat misleading. All repeaters are faster than a single-shot, but *in experienced hands*, a lever-action isn't necessarily faster than a bolt-action, and neither is as fast as a slide-action. In close-cover, fast-breaking situations it is probably desirable to have more than one shot available, but with practice any of the repeating actions is fast enough. Also misleading is the very nickname "brush cartridges." No cartridge, regardless of caliber, is particularly good at "busting brush." The advantage of the typical, slow-moving brush cartridges isn't to get through brush but rather to soundly anchor the game. This they do well.

The close-cover rifle may wear a low-power scope or it may sport open sights, depending on its intended use. As we've seen, it will probably be a repeater, most likely chambered to a fairly slow, large-caliber cartridge. It should probably be relatively short in the barrel, but first and foremost it must be responsive and fast-handling, just like a dangerous-game rifle.

Its primary capability should be to allow fast and accurate shooting at very short range, often on moving game. Its primary limitation is that it is a short-range affair.

GENERAL-PURPOSE RIFLES

If you live in Alaska and spend most of your time in willow thickets with brown bears, your "perfect rifle" may be a dangerous-game rifle. If you live in eastern Wyoming and your primary fall fare is pronghorn and deer on the plains, a long-range rifle may be just your ticket. If you're a backpack hunter, an ultra-lightweight may be the thing. If you stand-hunt big northern whitetails in dense hardwood thickets, you may feel most comfortable with a close-cover rifle. Most of us, however, are best served by a more versatile rifle—especially if we hunt a variety of game under a variety of conditions.

Even if there is no perfect all-round rifle, the vast majority of sporting rifles are actually quite versatile. The full range of action types can be used, and there are myriad cartridges to choose from—literally dozens of cartridges between, say, .25 and .33 caliber that offer a lot of flexibility. Your choice depends on what you hunt and what you might want to hunt, but any cartridge within this broad range that offers enough velocity to make hitting practical out to 250 or 300 yards offers the versatility you want.

Such a rifle can be wood- or synthetic-stocked. It will probably weigh, complete, from $7^{1}/_{2}$ to $8^{1}/_{2}$ pounds. Part of that weight is in the scope. Again, the choice there depends on your eyes, your comfort level, and the kind of hunting you do, but a truly versatile rifle *will be scoped*, and the scope may range from a fixed 4X on up to a variable of, say, 3.5-10X in power range.

The two Model 700 .30-06s that I chose to "work up" in the course of this book are very typical, but there are many, many potential choices. This "versatile rifle" is not a 500-yard rifle. It is not a good choice for stopping a charging grizzly. It is not ideal for sorting a black bear from a pack of dogs. It may get heavy on a two-week backpack sheep hunt. Mind you, it can do all of these things in a pinch. More importantly, however, it can be used effectively and with little compromise for most North American hunting under most conditions. You must decide whether you need a more specialized rifle for your hunting conditions, but I believe that most of us are best served by a versatile rifle well suited to a wide variety of hunting conditions.

differences really are subtle. With the proper chambering and sight equipment, each and every one of the six action types is adaptable to virtually any hunting application.

Although none of this has changed much in the last hundred years, let's briefly review the strengths and weaknesses of each action type.

DOUBLE RIFLES

Two-barreled rifles are extremely uncommon in America, although they retain significant followings in Europe and among hunters of dangerous game in both Africa and Asia. The double can be an over/under or a side-by-side design, and there are numerous variations of actions, differing in locking and unlocking mechanisms, spring arrangements, safeties, and such. The double is really a throwback to the muzzleloading era, when multiple barrels were the only means for obtaining a fast second shot.

Although not impressive by bolt-action standards, this 50-yard group from a double rifle is exceptional accuracy for this type of rifle. On the other hand, nothing is better than a double for stopping a charge, and raw accuracy is a very secondary consideration.

══ CHAPTER THREE ══

CHOOSE YOUR ACTION

Although there continue to be refinements and variations—some for the better and some not—all of the basic rifle actions available today have been around for more than a century. Even an effective—if not perfected—self-loading action existed before the turn of this century. Given this kind of history, it's unlikely that I can shed any new light on the advantages and disadvantages of the various action types! Besides, I've written about rifle actions elsewhere—several "elsewheres," to be more precise. This chapter should be considered a brief review, with more detailed information available in other writings, not only by myself but by a number of good modern gunwriters.

There are six basic rifle actions: single-shot, double-barreled, slide-action, lever-action, bolt-action, and semiautomatic or self-loading. Most shooters have their preferences, and sometimes these preferences and prejudices are strong. I certainly have mine, but it should be said right here that your decision in choosing the type of action for *your* rifle should be based primarily on what makes *you* the most comfortable and gives *you* the most confidence. There are definite differences among the action types, and we'll examine these subtleties while reviewing the various actions. Keep in mind that appearances and mechanical functioning may seem radically different from one action to another, but in practice the

I used a Heym double barrel in .500 Nitro Express to collect these tusks in Mozambique. That's what a double rifle is all about—fast shooting at close range, and the bigger the game, the better.

This is why the double remains popular for hunting dangerous game, and also why many European hunters rely on it for wild boar hunting: Consisting essentially of two separate firing mechanisms as well as two barrels, the double is unequaled in its ability to offer a fast, reliable second shot. This type of ultra-reliability and very rapid (though limited) firepower certainly has applications in North America. Several Alaskan brown bear guides use large-caliber doubles for backup work, and you could certainly make a good case for using a double rifle in an appropriate caliber for *any* close-cover work, from whitetails on up.

The double rifle does have some drawbacks. First is cost. A double rifle is actually a pretty simple firearm; metal and machining techniques have changed, but even the very finest modern doubles are based on 1880s design and technology. Unfortunately, it takes a lot of handwork to put a double together. The inletting is difficult and painstaking, and getting the two

In the right caliber and configuration, any of the action types are suitable for most hunting purposes. This slick little Winchester Model 88 chambered to .308 is a great deer rifle—but so is virtually any rifle chambered to .308 Winchester.

barrels to shoot together ("regulating") is time-consuming and expensive. A double rifle doesn't have to be fancy, but there is no such thing as a "production" double—all require a lot of handwork. Even fairly basic double rifles start in the thousands, many times more than factory rifles in all the other action types.

Even if cost is not an object, most double rifles are limited in accuracy. A very few shoot amazingly well, but it's impossible to get the two barrels to shoot exactly together at all ranges. Any double that groups *both barrels* within 4 inches at 100 yards is not only acceptable—it's superb. While this is adequate accuracy for any close-cover shooting, double rifles that shoot accurately enough for precise shot placement to 200 yards are very rare. Of course you can scope them, and of course they can be built in flat-shooting small and medium calibers as well as charge-stoppers. But you cannot consistently make medium- and long-range rifles out of them.

There is a lot of interest in double rifles today, with more being made than ever before—including a fair number of U.S. makers. The thing to keep in mind, despite their great charisma and genuine utility in close-range situations, is that a double rifle is not a versatile choice. Lastly, a double rifle cannot be

Although I've tried it and gotten away with it, I don't recommend the single-shot for dangerous game. No matter how hard you try, you can't always anchor game like Cape buffalo with one shot, and following them up isn't my idea of fun.

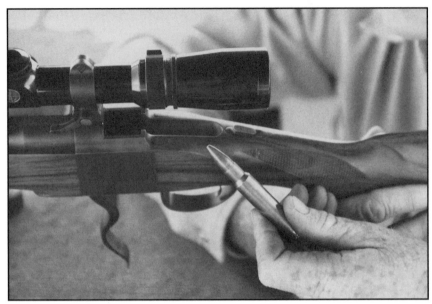

The appeal of the one-shot concept is very strong, and has much merit. This is a Dakota Model 10, a fine-looking semi-custom single shot offered in almost any chambering imaginable.

"under loaded" in the magazine; it is either fully loaded or fully empty. This makes a double slower in the field when you want to carry it unloaded.

SINGLE-SHOTS

The single-shot was virtually a dead issue when, about thirty years ago, Bill Ruger went way out on a limb and introduced the Ruger Number One. I don't know if its continued success has surprised Mr. Ruger, but it sure surprised all of us repeater-oriented rifle nuts!

As is the case with double rifles, there is wonderful appeal to the single-shot. Part of it is the nostalgia and the charm. Part, too, lies in the simplicity and wonderfully clean lines of a one-shooter. And then there's the undeniable appeal of "one shot, one animal." There is not a great proliferation of single-shot hunting rifles on the market, but the appeal is certainly strong enough to keep the Ruger Number One in business. In addition, Browning has its Hi-Wall and Lo-Wall falling blocks, Thompson/Center has adapted its break-open Contender action into carbine form, and Harrington & Richardson offers its good old top-lever break-open Topper action in several rifle chamberings. Dakota offers its lovely Model 10 in several action sizes, and quite a lot of custom rifle makers work with various single-shot actions.

There is nothing inherently wrong with choosing a single-shot. The actions are extremely strong; the Ruger especially is stout enough and big enough to house darn near any sporting cartridge you can think of, so chamberings are available for the full gamut of hunting use. I've carried a single-shot a good deal, including for use on dangerous game. One thing the single-shot does is make you very careful with that first shot—and that is not a bad thing!

With practice, it is possible to reload a single-shot very quickly. However, do not delude yourself into thinking that you can reload a single-shot as quickly as you can work a repeating action. I've tried real hard, and it just ain't possible. Of course, the idea behind the single-shot is to make that first shot count. Reality is that sometimes it's nice to have a second one! Under most circumstances, you can get that second shot into a single-shot action fast enough to do what needs to be done—but not always. Twice I've fumbled trying to reload a single-shot while a wounded Cape buffalo dashed into the bush. Both bulls, fortunately, quickly succumbed to the first shot. But after the brush closed around them and I had to follow the tracks to find out what I'd done—or not done—with that one shot, I was very nervous and felt more than a bit foolish. I don't think I'll use a single-shot on dangerous game again. I probably will use one again in a lot of other hunting applications, and if you wish to, you'll get no argument from me.

The strengths of the single-shot are: Simplicity—not necessarily mechanical but the ease of loading and unloading; lacking a repeating action, they are very short and handy, with barrel length equal to a repeater, and can be barreled long without excessive overall length; and finally, the very emphasis they place on that critical first shot.

I think single-shots also have three drawbacks. First is that same reliance on the one shot. It's a nice concept, but the lack of a readily available follow-up shot can in some instances lead to difficulty in recovering wounded game—or, with dangerous game, cause unnecessary hazards. Second, the single-shot is either fully loaded or fully empty. There is no easily accessible magazine, which is awkward on horseback hunts. You have to keep at least one cartridge *very* available, because you can't simply cycle the action and change a completely safe rifle to completely loaded. Third, most of the modern single-shots have two-piece stocks. While the single-shot action can be exceptionally accurate, it is much more difficult to bed a two-piece stock for optimum accuracy. Heavy barrels help, so you see a fair number of single-shot varminters, but you see very few long-range rifles built on two-piece-stock single-shots.

Harrington & Richardson's inexpensive break-open action is available in quite a few centerfire chamberings these days. Plain and simple, it's a fine rifle.

This is the Browning BLR in .358. Like the Savage 99, Winchester 88, and a few others, the BLR has a box magazine so it can handle spitzer bullets. The BLR is offered in long-action form, and is the only lever action ever chambered to belted magnums.

SLIDE-ACTION

Once very popular, the slide-action centerfire seemed nearly doomed until very recently. For some years now the last slide-action hunting rifle on the market was the Remington 760 series, but in 1997 Browning modified its BAR receiver into slide-action operation, the Browning Pump Rifle (BPR). Though it doesn't take a rocket scientist to figure that this move was at least partially based on concern that semiautomatic sporters would be legislated into obsolescence, the new BPR has, at least initially, been very popular.

One very new wrinkle to the BPR, by the way, has been its availability in .300 Winchester Magnum, the first slide-action ever offered in a belted magnum. If the BPS .300 continues to be successful, Browning may well add the .338. The Remington is limited to the .30-06 case head, with .35 Whelen the most powerful chambering in which it has ever been offered. With Browning's Magnum pump gun, it could be argued that there are now slide-actions for any and every North American hunting venue. So why not a slide-action?

No reason at all. The slide-action in experienced hands is the very fastest manual repeating action. Any slide-action (or lever, or semiauto) will be a bit more finicky in its diet than the average bolt-action, but I would give its manually operated bolt a reliability edge over a semiauto, and it's nearly as fast. Actually, it could be faster. Exhibition shotgunners almost invariably favor slide-action shotguns over semiautos, simply because they can manually cycle a well-broken-in slide-action much faster than a semiauto!

The stronghold of the slide-action lies with the deep-woods whitetail hunters, especially Pennsylvanians (who, by law, cannot use semiautomatics). Although we tend to think of slide-actions as not particularly accurate, this is not altogether true. I have shot a number of Remingtons that were *very* accurate, and since the BPR shares the BAR's receiver, and most BARs shoot well, I'd be surprised if the BPR wasn't, on average, plenty accurate for most hunting use. The two-piece stock does remain a limitation for realizing extreme accuracy, and it's very difficult to get a good, crisp trigger pull out of a slide-action. It also lacks the primary extraction leverage of the bolt-action, so will generally feed most reliably with factory loads. However, for general hunting use the only real limitation to the slide-action is the small selection of both models and calibers.

SEMIAUTOMATIC

A buddy of mine, Colorado outfitter Lad Shunneson, has a badly battered Browning BAR chambered to .300 Winchester Magnum. The outside metal is Teflon-coated, and the stock wears worn and partly peeled camouflage tape. The rifle looks like hell, and Lad swears he has never cleaned it. I don't know if that's

The Valmet semiauto is actually based on the AK-47 (Kalashnikov) action. Like most rifles of any action type, with good barrels and good ammo it shoots quite well.

true, but I do know that he has used this rifle all over the world. In fact, the only time I've ever seen him use anything else was when local hunting regulations prohibited use of a self-loader. He shoots the rifle very well, and has a whole houseful of trophies to prove it. Every time we get together, Lad waxes eloquent on the advantages of his "modern rifle," all the while casting aspersions on my manually operated and obsolescent rifle— regardless of its make or model.

The modern semiauto, whether Remington, Browning, or whatever, works well. I have enough experience with both military and civilian self-loaders that I do not question their reliability. They can also be very accurate. I've seen both Brownings and Remingtons that shot wonderfully, and of course match-barreled rifles like the M1A and H-Bar AR 15 can work wonders.

All that said, and Lad's success aside, the semiautomatic is not my idea of a hunting rifle. If it's yours, though, that's just fine. The two-piece stock on most sporting models makes optimizing accuracy more difficult. Too, the semiautomatic is the most finicky eater of the action types. You can handload for them, but it's more difficult.

Actually, the semiauto really isn't a handloader's rifle, not only because of the care in sizing and seating to ensure cycling, but also because you have to do a lot of scrabbling around to recover the

Lever-action, slide-action, single-shot, semiauto, bolt-action—all very versatile. Of all the action types, only the double rifle is almost universally a short-range, special purpose arm because of its limited accuracy.

This is a Winchester Model 71 in .348, a "traditional" lever-action. Although this cartridge is actually pretty fast, the tubular magazine requires flat-point bullets. They hit hard, but poor aerodynamics limit the range on this type of lever-action regardless of chambering.

brass. However, the modern semiauto is accurate enough, and reliable enough, and of course it's very fast for repeat shots. Model and caliber selections are limited, but Browning's chamberings go up to .338 Winchester Magnum, so there is a semiauto for everything on this continent up to the big bears.

Provided you aren't a dedicated handloader, drawbacks are actually few. The primary one, to me, is that it's noisy to load a semiauto. To ensure functioning, you can't "baby" the bolt; you need to let it snap forward, which is noisy. It's also noisy, though less so, to unload the chamber. This means that in the still of the morning in a treestand—or when you've almost completed a stalk in rough country and it's time to get the rifle ready for action—you are stuck with that loud mechanical *clack* when you load your chamber. I much prefer the action types that can be loaded and unloaded slowly and quietly, this because I rarely carry a round in the chamber when I'm on the move . . . especially in rough country.

LEVER-ACTION

Although there are several makes and models of the all-American lever-action, there are really two *types* of lever-action rifle. One is the "traditional" lever, mostly tubular magazine rifles, chambered to the so-called "brush cartridges." No, they don't really bust brush any better than anything else, but they use flat-point bullets that are as aerodynamic as rocks . . . and hit like freight trains. When we think of this type of rifle, we're usually thinking of Winchester '92s, '94s, '86s, and such, and the Marlin 336 series. To this group should also be added the new Ruger .44 Magnum lever-action. One thing that these rifles have in common is that they are fairly short-range affairs—and also fast-handling and effective. Most (excluding the Ruger) have the same two-piece-stock accuracy bugaboo, but this really isn't a problem. They shoot plenty well enough for the short ranges at which they are best suited. I happen to like this type of rifle very much, and have absolutely no argument with anyone who chooses one . . . provided the range limitations are acceptable.

I also like the other type of lever-action. This one not only uses some sort of box magazine, enabling the use of aerodynamic spitzer bullets, but is also chambered to relatively fast and flat-shooting cartridges. There are just three that I can think of right now: Savage 99, Browning BLR, and the reintroduced Winchester '95. Both the Browning and the Winchester chamber .30-06-length cartridges, with the Browning even offered in belted magnums. The Savage is restricted to .308-length cartridges, but there's certainly nothing wrong with the .308 Winchester as a very versatile hunting cartridge.

All three of these rifles share the two-piece stock that we've discussed previously. The Savage and Winchester '95 are both rear-locking, which also tends to restrict accuracy a bit. None of them have the extraction power of a bolt-action and so are a bit more finicky in their diet, and although the '95 is a wonderfully nostalgic piece, it isn't designed for conventional scope mounting. No longer in production, and

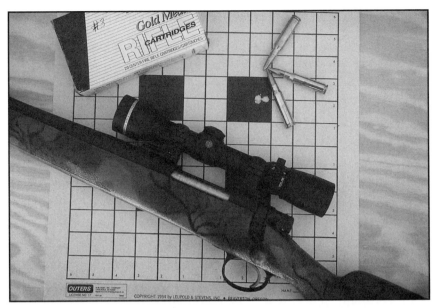

With its one-piece stock, rigid action, and forward-locking bolt, the typical bolt-action is the most accurate on average. It is also offered in the greatest number of models, chamberings, and configurations. This is a Harris Gunworks short-action .308.

more's the pity, are the Sako Finnwolf and Winchester Model 88, both *one-piece-stock* lever-actions with box magazines and forward-locking bolts.

I have barely laid eyes on the Sako—they're rare—but I've used several Model 88s and have seen some that were customized with good stocks and top-quality barrels. Potential accuracy is absolutely amazing, and blows all kinds of holes in the old story about lever-actions not shooting well. On the other hand, I've also had Savage 99s and Browning BLRs that were real tackdrivers—and I've still got a Winchester Model 94 in .30-30 that will shoot ¾-inch groups at 100 yards all day long—with an aperture sight! So I'm not selling the lever-action short. Normal accuracy plus chambering limitations keep them out of the serious long-range arena, but if you like lever guns there are models and calibers that fit in just about anywhere else.

BOLT-ACTION

I am not as much a bolt-action fan as you might think. My field experience with both slide-actions and semiautomatics is fairly limited, but I have hunted quite a lot with single-shots, lever-actions, and double rifles—and will probably continue to do so. It is not purely accidental, however, that the "project rifles" I have chosen to use throughout this book are bolt-actions. All of the action types, in proper chamberings and with appropriate sights and loads, can provide good service in most hunting applications, but there should be little question that the bolt-action is the most versatile hunting rifle action. This is why the bolt-action is the dominant action worldwide. All of the others have their following and are certainly functional, but for at least the last half-century the bolt-action has been the most prevalent sporting rifle action. I seriously doubt that this will change in the foreseeable future.

There are many good reasons this is so. The bolt-action is not necessarily the strongest action; the falling-block single-shot is also incredibly strong. However, it is certainly strong enough and, more importantly, is easily adapted to cartridges that span the full range of hunting needs. It also possesses the strongest camming power for extraction and so is the least finicky about the loads it will accept. It is the most *consistently* accurate action. A particular rifle in any action type, even a double, may be more accurate than a particular bolt-action, but on average the bolt-action will win the accuracy race against any other action type. This is because its rigid receiver and strong lockup are conducive to accuracy, and because its typical one-piece stock is stable and relatively simple to bed.

In these days of product liability paranoia, virtually all factory rifles are supplied with truly horrible trigger pulls—much too heavy and generally creepy as well. So it's not correct to say that bolt-actions have better trigger pulls. It is correct to say that most bolt-actions have triggers that can be readily adjusted to crisp, clean pulls—even though a gunsmith's services may be needed. If bolt-action triggers cannot be adjusted, they can usually be replaced. This is often not the case with the triggers of other action types. It is extremely difficult, and often quite unsafe, to mess with the trigger of a semiauto, slide-action, or lever-action. In most models you simply have to learn to deal with the factory trigger, which you can do . . . but a heavy, creepy trigger is the single most serious detriment to realizing your rifle's accuracy potential.

For the purposes of this book I have chosen to use bolt-actions as we go through the various steps of choosing and mounting a scope, checking bedding, selecting loads, and so forth. This may seem to imply that I am recommending that *you* select a bolt-action. Such a supposition isn't altogether untrue. I do believe the bolt is the most versatile and most adaptable action, as well as being the most "on-average" accurate. In most shooters' hands it is a bit slower to operate than the other repeating actions, but with practice a bolt-action can be very fast—certainly fast enough. I don't know your predominant hunting conditions. Your needs may be perfectly satisfied by a good old .30-30 lever-action, and that's fine. You may prefer the self-discipline of a single-shot, and that's fine as well. You may be a serious bird hunter who wants a deer rifle as similar as possible to your slide-action or semiautomatic shotgun, and that's fine, too. *All* of the action types can be superb hunting rifles—but none of them is suitable without proper cartridges, appropriate sights, and gun fit that's right for you.

CHAPTER FOUR

AVOIDING CARTRIDGE CONFUSION

Guys like me—gunwriting hacks—make a fairly large portion of our incomes waxing eloquent about the relative virtues of one cartridge or another. The same kind of comparison keeps many a campfire discussion lively until the wee hours. This is good. I need things to write about, and we all need wholesome and interesting topics to hash out by the fire. A good cartridge debate is a very healthy thing; if you don't have enough confidence in your cartridge to champion it against all comers, then you'd better find one you can argue in favor of!

Cartridge comparisons are lots of fun and always interesting. Generally speaking, they do little harm, but if you happen to be a newcomer to the game, it can get downright confusing. There are dozens and dozens of commercial cartridges suitable for big-game hunting, and many of them are very similar. You're in for a very difficult task if you seek the "perfect" cartridge for your hunting. Chances are good that at least a half-dozen cartridges will fill the bill nicely . . . and chances are very poor that there is just *one* cartridge that stands out as "perfect."

A detailed ballistic analysis is beyond the scope of this book, as is a detailed discussion of the best cartridges for various types of game and hunting. You can find entire books on the subject (including some of mine!), and all of the bullet and ammunition manufacturers offer very clear, easy-to-read ballistics charts that offer an excellent basis for comparison. Actually, however, it's very possible that the more

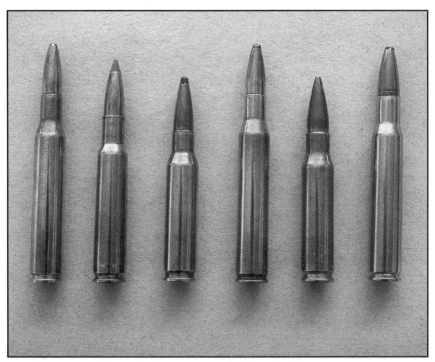

Left to right: .270 Winchester, 7x57, 7mm-08 Remington, .280 Remington, .308 Winchester, .30-06. You could argue that the .30-06 is better for larger game and the .270 is better in open country, but under most circumstances versatile cartridges like these could be used interchangeably and neither the shooter nor the game would know the difference.

reading you do the more confused you will become! One writer champions the .270, another the .280, another the .30-06, and still another the 7mm Remington Magnum. You like what "writer .280" has to say, but when you look at the ballistics charts you find that although the .280 is neither the fastest nor the flattest, there isn't much difference among the four. How can you determine the best choice?

In most cases you can't, because there is no "best" choice. On the other hand, there probably isn't a "wrong" choice, either. If you are a deer hunter in country that ranges from fairly thick to fairly open, any of these cartridges will work very well. You could confuse things even more by adding the 7mm-08 Remington, 7x57 Mauser, 7x64, .308 Winchester, and perhaps two dozen more cartridges that are a little bigger, a little smaller, a little slower, or a little faster . . . and you *still* couldn't make a wrong choice.

If you're a deer hunter, shooting normal-sized deer at normal ranges (whatever that is!), there is a huge selection of cartridges between about .270 and about .30 in caliber that will work very well. In fact, if you had several rifles that were identical except in chambering, you could probably shoot them interchangeably and neither you nor the deer would ever know the difference. Caliber selection is not rocket science; we have many good choices, and much overlap.

There are several things to keep in mind. First, the very basics. Although I try to be precise in my language, I'm not perfect—and much writing on the subject can be very confusing. "Cartridge" and "caliber" are not interchangeable terms. A cartridge is a complete round of ammunition—case, bullet, propellant charge, and powder. Caliber, on the other hand, refers only to the interior dimensions of a rifle's barrel—and to a matching bullet diameter. The confusing thing is that, based on differing case dimensions, there may be (and probably are) several *cartridges* in any given *caliber*. For instance, you want

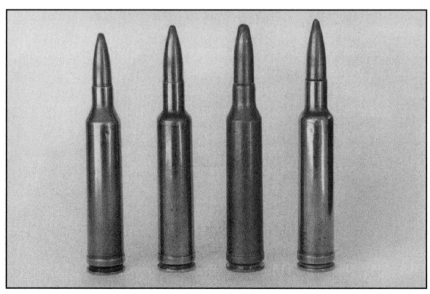

Left to right: .264 Winchester Magnum, .270 Weatherby Magnum, 7mm Remington Magnum, 7mm Weatherby Magnum. These are true magnums, meaning they are much faster than an existing cartridge of the same caliber. All are fine open-country cartridges.

to buy a rifle in caliber .270. OK, but *which* .270, the .270 Winchester or .270 Weatherby Magnum? Both of these *cartridges* are .270s, but they are not interchangeable, and there's a big difference in case dimensions and resulting velocities.

It's more confusing in caliber .30, with numerous cartridges to choose from. It gets even worse if you try to figure out exactly what a cartridge's name actually *means*. Bullet diameters and case dimensions are real. Cartridges, however, are usually introduced by manufacturers who want to make money by selling them . . . so the names can be misleading. Neither .270, for instance, is *really* a .270; both use .277-inch bullets, so the ".270" designation is not precise. In caliber .30, you have (among others) the .30-30 Winchester, .307 Winchester, .30-06 Springfield, .308 Winchester, and .300 Winchester Magnum. All of these cartridges shoot bullets with a diameter of .308 inches—but each has different case dimensions and differing levels of performance. Even so, this is pretty straightforward in the world of cartridge designations. It gets worse.

Without getting too technical, a rifled barrel has two diameters—groove to groove, and land to land. Bullet diameter generally matches groove diameter; the lands engrave into the bullet to impart the stabilizing spin, but the bullet must fill the bore from groove to groove to block the expanding gas. Most cartridges are named by a reasonable approximation of bullet (or groove) diameter. Both the .338 Winchester and .340 Weatherby Magnums, for instance, use .338-inch bullets. Roy Weatherby often "offset" his cartridge designations by a few thousandths to separate them from "standard" cartridges of like caliber: His .378 uses .375-inch bullets, his .460 uses .458-inch bullets, and so forth. That's easy. The British—and a few others from time to time—ignored groove and bullet diameter and named many cartridges by *land* diameter. This can be really confusing. In that fashion, the British call most 6.5mm cartridges (bullet diameter .264) a ".256"—not the same as our .25 caliber, which uses a .257-inch bullet. The British designation for the 7x57 Mauser (bullet diameter .284, like all the 7mms) is .275—but that ain't the same as our .270.

I used a .270 Winchester, a classic mountain cartridge, to take this fine bighorn ram. It was a traditional and acceptable choice, but many cartridges would have done just as well.

Most cartridge designations start with something that refers to the caliber, or diameter—even if it isn't exact. This isn't always consistent. Weatherby's new .30-378, for instance, is a .30-caliber cartridge based on the big .378 Weatherby case. Simple. Except that the British convention is to name the parent case first, followed by the diameter. Thus the new .500-.416 Nitro Express is the .500 NE case necked down to accept a .416-inch bullet! Metric cartridges are generally the simplest to understand and the most exact. The 7x57 Mauser is a 7mm (.284) cartridge fired from a case that's 57 millimeters in length, and the firm of Mauser introduced the cartridge. The 7x64 Brenneke is another 7mm cartridge, but this one uses a 64-millimeter case, and Wilhelm Brenneke was its designer.

American designations can be a bit more difficult to figure. Many of our older cartridges—.30-30, .30-40, .45-70—are carryovers from

The .338 Winchester Magnum used by Nosler Bullets' Chub Eastman is an extremely versatile cartridge. Larger than needed for smaller game, it's a very fine "all-round" choice if your hunting includes game larger than deer.

the blackpowder days. The first number is the caliber, but the second number is the "standard" weight of the blackpowder charge used more than a century ago! There are anomalies, too: The "06" in .30-06 was an abbreviation to differentiate the slightly modified 1906 version from the 1903 version.

Only slightly more consistency exists in the word or words appended to the numbers. Most common is for a cartridge to be named for its designer, or for the company that introduced it. Either way, these words are extremely important in differentiating cartridges of like caliber. For instance, the .35 Remington (introduced by Remington) uses a much smaller case than the .35 Whelen (also introduced by Remington but named after Col. Townsend Whelen). Remember that cartridge designations *must* identify a cartridge well enough to prevent a mismatch—but it's also OK if they have the "sizzle" to help sell the cartridge.

Sometimes this is good fun, but sometimes it's misleading. In the former category are whimsical names such as John Lazzeroni uses for his red-hot cartridges: Firehawk, Scramjet, Warbird, etc. As a name, I particularly like A-Square's .338 Excalibur. The cartridge is a fast, heavy-recoiling, large-cased .338. Excalibur was, of course, King Arthur's sword, and A-Square's boss is Art Alphin. Cute. Not so cute, to me, is the overuse of buzzwords like "magnum" and "express."

A couple of decades back we were magnum-crazy. Virtually every cartridge introduced in the late 1950s and early 1960s had a magnum suffix. Now, at least in its pure sense, magnum means bigger than standard. Originally it applied to a big bottle of champagne, and in the blackpowder era the British applied it to extra-large cartridge cases. The magnum designation has been used far too much, but it does generally mean "faster." The questions you should always ask when considering a magnum are "faster than what?" and "why?" The

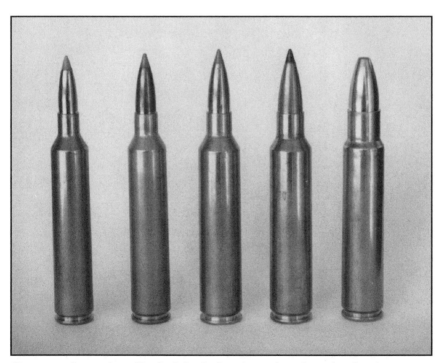

"Proprietary" cartridges, offered only by the firm that makes rifles so chambered, are coming back. This is the Lazzeroni family of unbelted magnums: 6.53 Scramjet; 7.21 Firehawk; 7.82 Warbird; 8.59 Titan; 10.57 Meteor.

various .30 calibers with magnum designations—H&H, Norma, Winchester, Weatherby—are all faster than the .30-06 and the .308 Winchester. All will deliver more velocity and energy, and all will shoot flatter. So you must then ask, "Why do I need the extra performance (and noise, recoil, and gun weight)?" Maybe you do and maybe you don't, but faster and bigger aren't always better.

Sometimes magnum is a bit misleading. The short-cased (and short-lived!) 6.5mm Remington Magnum wasn't faster than some number of European 6.5mm cartridges, and it had no American counterpart to be a "magnum" of. That was stretching the point; the

Left to right: .308 Winchester, .30-06, .300 Winchester Magnum, .300 Weatherby Magnum. These are all .30-calibers, but each is an altogether different cartridge, with slightly different hunting uses.

ancient 6.5x55 is just as good a cartridge. Not to pick on Remington, but I don't understand what is magnum about its .416 Remington Magnum. It's a fine cartridge, duplicating the ballistics of the time-honored .416 Rigby but in a much more compact case. The Rigby, by the way, has never been called a magnum—and there has never been a smaller or slower cartridge for either to be a magnum version of. Now, the .416 Weatherby Magnum uses the same .416 bullets but at greatly increased velocity. That's a "real" magnum. On the other hand, the .416 Remington/Rigby velocity has been considered adequate since 1912, so why do you need the extra velocity? Maybe you do and maybe you don't. Make sure you know the real capabilities of any cartridge you're considering—not just the hype—and be certain this is what you need.

Every ammunition manufacturer's catalog will have excellent ballistics tables that are very good for comparing cartridges. Reloading manuals generally offer even more detailed data and so are extremely useful even if you don't handload. Keep in mind that ballistics tables aren't perfect. They do tend to be pretty accurate these days, but they are based on data obtained from a given test rifle. Your rifle may have a shorter or longer barrel, a tighter or looser bore or chamber, etc., so you can't consider printed ballistics data as Gospel—but it's plenty close enough to make fair comparisons.

A study of such tables will tell you that, given careful bullet selection, there is very little *practical* difference at normal game ranges—out to 300 yards or so—between such versatile hunting cartridges as the .270 Winchester, .280 Remington, 7mm Remington Magnum, and .30-06. Mind you, this "general purpose" cartridge is not the only type of hunting cartridge worth considering. In chapter 2 we discussed several types of specialized hunting rifles, and it shouldn't be surprising that a sort of "family" of cartridges goes along with each.

If you're considering purchasing a long-range rifle, then you probably want a long-range cartridge to go with it. Such cartridges have large powder capacity relative to caliber, and will produce high velocity, which in turn yields flat trajectory and high energy retention. As is always the case, caliber depends upon the game to be hunted. The pronghorn or open-country deer hunter may

High velocity isn't always the best course. A low-velocity "brush" cartridge like the old .348 with heavy, blunt-nosed bullets hits hard and anchors game. It's a fine choice on tough game at close range.

prefer a small-caliber magnum like the .257 or .270 Weatherby Magnums, or the .264 Winchester Magnum, or any of the faster 7mm magnums. A serious elk hunter might choose a fast .33, while those in search of the most versatile long-range rig will usually choose a hot .30 caliber.

Dangerous-game rifles must be chambered to cartridges appropriate for the game. This generally starts with the .375 H&H, but a rifle intended for use on elephant will probably chamber a much larger cartridge. Close-cover rifles may also be chambered to cartridges that are large in caliber, but will probably be much slower and perhaps shoot lighter bullets than a dangerous-game rifle. For instance, the 125-year-old .45-70 is a wonderful and still-popular "brush cartridge." It is not a dangerous-game cartridge. The .458 Winchester Magnum, also a .45 caliber, shoots a heavier bullet much faster than the .45-70 is capable of, and is adequate for any game on earth.

Ultra-lightweights really don't have a specific family of cartridges. Depending on how much recoil you're willing to accept, virtually any cartridge can be built into a light—or lighter than normal—rifle. However, the most likely candidates for very light rifles are short-cased cartridges that will function in shorter (and thus lighter) actions. The family of cartridges based on the .308 Winchester case—.243 Winchester, .260, and 7mm—'08 Remington, and .358 Winchester— best characterize this class of cartridge.

And then there are the very versatile, general-purpose, "all-round" hunting cartridges. I keep going back to the quartet formed by the .270 Winchester, .280 Remington, .30-06 Springfield, and 7mm Remington Magnum to illustrate this group, but they are not the only very versatile cartridges. To this list one could certainly add the 7x57 Mauser, the .308 Winchester, and the magnum .30s—and probably a whole lot more. All of the cartridges on this list will do just about anything *most* hunters need to do.

You will note that I have chosen the .30-06 for my "project rifles." This is not accidental, any more so than the choice of the bolt-action. There are faster, flatter-shooting, more powerful, and inherently more accurate cartridges than the .30-06. However, no cartridge is offered in so great a variety of loads and bullet weights, and though there are several cartridges that are very versatile, I can't think of anything more versatile than the good old '06. This does not mean it should be your choice. The .270, .280, and 7mm magnums are a bit better in open country. The magnum .30s kick more but offer a bit more range and will handle heavy bullets better if you hunt larger game. If you live in Alaska, you might want to bypass my list altogether and look at a .338.

Some cartridges have tremendous potential but limited availability in factory ammo. For instance, the .280 Remington is a wonderful cartridge. Technically, it's the best of the indomitable triad formed by the .270, .280, and .30-06. But factory loads are very limited, so if you don't handload, it's a questionable choice. Factory loads for the good old 7x57 are generally very mild, intended for use in *all* 7x57s, even very old rifles. With a modern rifle and good handloads, the 7x57 stands right up there with the .270, .280, and .30-06. If you don't handload, it's *still* a good cartridge—but not in the same league.

So don't interpret my use of the .30-06 as implying that this is always the best choice. It's rarely a bad choice, but it's far from the only solution to the caliber dilemma, and it may not be the best choice for you. Just make certain that you've evaluated all the considerations—ammo availability, the recoil level you're comfortable with, the game you hunt, and the kind of country you hunt—before you make your decision. It's almost impossible to make a wrong choice, but some cartridges are almost certainly better than others for your needs!

CHAPTER FIVE

NEW, USED, OR CUSTOM?

As we've already discussed, I have obtained two rifles that we'll be seeing a lot more of in chapters to come. One is a brand-new Remington 700, and I assume it was selected at random off the assembly line. It isn't true—or at least isn't often true—that the major manufacturers "cherry pick" the guns they send to writers. Nor is it necessary. Most new guns work well—but I've seen some very bizarre things in the way of test guns. There was a .22 rifle that wasn't rifled at all, and there have been feeding, extraction, and ejection problems, and . . . well, anything is possible. But I will assume that the new Model 700, still in its box at this writing, will work. I also assume that it will shoot reasonably well, although just how well is something we will see. "Lemons" are possible with any make or model, but I will also say that with any new rifle from a major manufacturer, you can make these assumptions: It will work, and it will shoot reasonably well.

The other Model 700 was picked straight off a used-gun rack at Bridges' Sports Shop, our local Paso Robles gunshop. I don't know who owned it previously or how much it has been shot. The barrel looks fine, but there's a fair amount of surface rust on the bolt and barrel. The gun has been used, and hasn't been well taken care of. As is the case with the new rifle, I have no idea how it will shoot—but it isn't that old or that worn, and I expect that it will shoot OK.

So we have one brand-new rifle and one very typical used rifle. A third option is to have a custom rifle built. What route should you take when selecting *your* hunting rifle? I can't tell you, but I can give you a couple of rules of thumb. The first rule applies to used rifles: Never forget that there is a reason it's for sale! Unless you know the person selling it, you can't know the exact reason . . . and even if you know that person, can you trust him? Whether horse-trading or gun-trading, the prevailing law is "let the buyer beware."

I have sold and traded a lot of rifles over the years, and I've let go of some guns that I sure wish I'd kept. Some went because I needed cash. Others went because I wanted to trade up, in either caliber or quality. Still others have gone away because the caliber was redundant of other rifles I owned. These are innocent reasons. Many good guns go on the rack because of death, divorce, or other natural causes. These, too, are innocent reasons.

Many guns also go on the used-gun rack for more insidious reasons—a barrel that is becoming shot-out, or a barrel that never shot well in the first place and its owner got tired of messing with it. I well recall a wonderful high-grade 28-gauge double that I had. The gun fit me like a dream, and I shot many quail with it. Then one day I had it on the skeet range and couldn't buy a target with the left barrel. I took it to the pattern board, and that barrel printed way low and left. I quickly sold it, and with no explanation. The guy who bought it was just as happy as I had been. I only hope he never takes it skeet shooting!

Many magnums are quickly sold because the owner decided recoil wasn't fun. Some are sold because the cartridge they chamber is dropped or becomes hard to find. Under such circumstances, the adage "one man's meat is another man's poison" applies. I would love to have been in Nairobi in the early 1960s with a bit of cash in my pocket; in those days one could have bought truckloads of fine old Mausers and double

Shopping for a used rifle is always risky, but there are bargains out there. The one thing you usually can't know is exactly why a used rifle is for sale. This is the used gun rack that I purchased the Model 700 ADL .30-06 from—and it proved a very good buy.

Factory rifles run the gamut from very plain to very fancy. This is the Savage Model 111, a very plain, attractively priced rifle that can usually be counted on to shoot extremely well.

rifles when Kynoch discontinued the big Nitro Express cartridges! Under such circumstances there can be real bargains . . . but with any used rifle the problem is always knowing exactly what you're getting into.

Under the best of circumstances, a used rifle has its barrel already broken in, the action has been smoothed with use, and the previous owner has worked all the bugs out of it. You may even get a decent scope more or less "thrown-in." Under the worst circumstances, you're buying somebody else's problems. Unless you know the seller or the deal is really good, you're generally better off buying a used gun from a reputable gunshop. If possible, take the rifle on some sort of approval and immediately take it to the range and see what you're getting into.

Now, even if it shoots terribly, it may still be a good deal. That depends on the price. Having a rifle rebarreled with a normal commercial barrel chambered to a standard cartridge is not very expensive—but if you can't trial-shoot the rifle, you'd best factor the cost of a new barrel into the price and see if it's still less than a new rifle of similar characteristics!

How about a custom rifle? When we think about "custom," we generally think of something that is made entirely and expressly to the customer's specifications. With rifles, however, there are varying degrees of "custom," and there's also such a thing as "semi-custom."

You can, for instance, get a barreled action and fit it into an aftermarket fiberglass stock and call that a "custom rifle."

If you want to call it that, it's fine with me—but it isn't really a made-to-order gun. You can also get a well-stocked, well-appointed rifle from one of several smaller manufacturers and dictate many of its specifications. This is what I call "semi-custom," or, if you prefer, "semi-production." This is the business that smaller makers like Dakota, Ultra Light Arms, A-Square, Lazzeroni Arms, and many others are in. They have basic models, but within that framework you have a wide range of calibers, stock dimensions, sights, finishes, and such to choose from.

Then there's a genuine custom rifle. Even this term almost never means that the riflesmith will make the entire rifle from scratch. A few—Kenny Jarrett and Bill Wiseman, to name two—make their own barrels. Others, like Fred Wells, make their own actions. Many make their own stocks, but just as many (especially those who specialize in synthetics) source their stocks from elsewhere. But whether

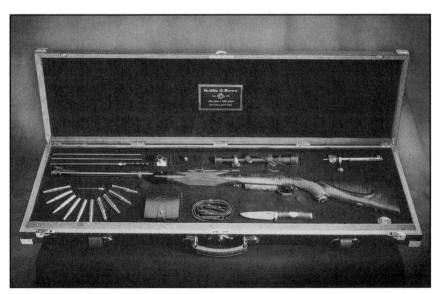

Custom rifles also run the gamut from plain to very ornate, with the sky as the limit. This is a lovely .416 Rigby built by Griffin & Howe for auction by the Safari Club. Rifles like this, though functional, are truly works of art and are rarely taken afield.

your chosen 'smith makes or sources the basic components, a custom rifle is designed specifically to your needs, from muzzle to buttplate.

The real tricks to ordering a custom rifle are to know what you want and then to find a custom maker whose general tastes are similar to yours. Custom gunmakers are artists. If you like Picasso, don't purchase a Rembrandt. If you like fine wood, go to a gunmaker who works with fine wood; if you want a synthetic stock, don't go to a gunmaker who works primarily in wood. If you find a like-minded gunmaker, chances are your primary concern will be the little things— checkering pattern, barrel length and contour, chambering, stock dimensions. This is happiness. Unhappiness is wanting something altogether different from the guns the maker normally turns out.

There are very good reasons for going the custom route. Some makers, like Kenny Jarrett, turn out rifles that are more accurate than anything you can buy off the shelf. Others, like David Miller, turn out rifles that are more beautiful than anything you can buy off the shelf. Some, like Kerry O'Day of Match Grade Arms and Mel Forbes of Ultra Light Arms, make very light rifles that also shoot extremely well. But it must be said that factory rifles today are very good—and are also offered in a bewildering array of stock styles, finishes, and specifications.

Although he is best known for his Beanfield Rifles, Kenny Jarrett also builds conventional sporters, usually with synthetic stocks. Like the Beanfield, there's one thing you can count on: A Jarrett rifle is going to shoot.

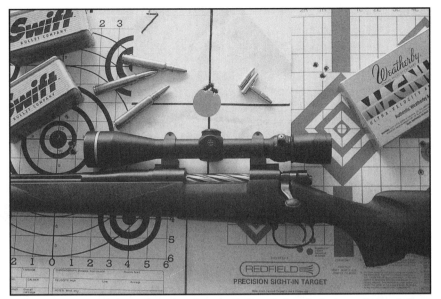

This .340 was made by Rich Reiley of High-Tech in Colorado Springs. Reiley believes that reliability and performance are of primary importance, and this rifle bears it out. It's one of the sweetest-shooting big rifles I've ever handled.

There is tremendous satisfaction in owning a custom rifle. I have a John Rigby .416, a Kenny Jarrett .30-06, a David Miller 7mm magnum, a Rogue River 8mm, and a couple of other "name" rifles. These are my most prized possessions, and I would never try to talk anyone out of the great pleasure that comes from owning such a piece. *But* I cannot tell you that my John Rigby .416 is ten times more reliable than an over-the-counter Remington, Ruger, or Winchester .416 would be. Or that my Jarrett .30-06 is six times more accurate than the Remington ADL that's sitting in the box beside me. The price differentials do not represent a similar difference in accuracy or reliability. What a custom rifle is all about is pride of ownership.

A custom rifle may or may not be more accurate than an off-the-shelf new *or* used rifle—that depends on how lucky you are, or perhaps how much extra work you put into the bedding and finding the right load. A custom rifle may or may not be more

Although they're wonderful, you can't say that a custom rifle like a David Miller is twenty times better than a factory rifle costing one-twentieth as much. On the other hand, when the chips are down, there's nothing like the confidence that a true custom rifle offers.

dependable than an off-the-shelf rifle—to some extent that factor depends on *you*. We'll come back to that subject. However, that pride of ownership business isn't all conceit.

Though you cannot buy five or ten or twenty times more accuracy or reliability in a custom rifle, you can buy an immeasurable and unquantifiable amount of confidence. A rifle that is truly built for you may not shoot better or function better than an off-the-shelf rifle. It darn well *should* fit you better . . . but you can make a factory gun fit without spending several thousand dollars on a custom rifle. What you cannot get in a production rifle, new or used, is that matchless feeling of having a rifle that is *you*, that was built to your specifications and to your tastes and is an extension of yourself—much like a portrait or sculpture of yourself.

A custom rifle is an ultimate conceit, an expression of vanity and ego . . . but in the field, when the chips are down, the small measure of added confidence that such a rifle gives you can be worth a very great deal. And in the field, even when things aren't going so well, just carrying and admiring that rifle can bring a great deal of pleasure. So I will not try to talk you out of buying a custom rifle. I will also not try to talk you into commissioning one. That's up to you, and it depends a lot on your budget, the amount of time you spend in the field, and your personal tastes.

Two final things on the subject: First, a custom rifle is not necessary to get everything you need out of a hunting rifle. Second, should you decide to go the custom route, there is no substitute for the special feeling you get from hunting with a rifle that is not only uniquely yours but also uniquely *you*.

Now, let's return to the subject of reliability. Rifles are a lot like automobiles. Although it may tick you off beyond description, when you buy a car you generally expect it to have some little bugs that require a trip to the dealer to correct. Firearms are not nearly as complex as cars, but the analogy is sound. Whether new, used, or custom, firearms often have

Lex Webernick of Rifles, Inc. is another performance-minded custom maker. Leica's Terry Moore, bottom right, was using a Rifles, Inc. in .280 and I was using a Rifles, Inc. in .300 Weatherby when we took these two South Dakota mule deer.

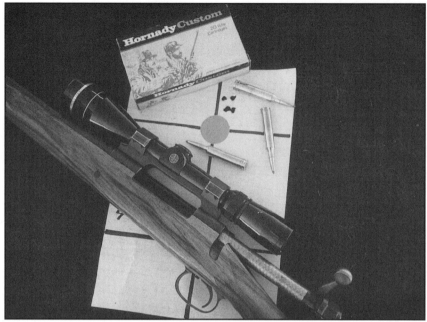

This is my David Miller 7mm Remington Magnum with a typical factory-ammo group. One of the unique features about the Miller rifle is the scope harness; this rifle hasn't changed a bit in the dozen years I've owned it.

little bugs that need to be worked out. Rich Reiley, the proprietor of a good Colorado Springs-based custom shop called High-Tech, phoned the other day and railed about an article in which the author had gone through a litany of problems with a custom rifle. According to Reiley, that was all wrong. A custom rifle shouldn't have such problems. OK, that's true—*but sometimes they do.*

Again, whether new, used, or custom, before you head to the field with a rifle, you simply must check it out from butt to muzzle, including all the mechanical functions. I hate to tell tales out of school, but I have unbelievable problems with rifles. Mind you, since much of what I do is write about guns, I've probably worked with more rifles than the average guy. What I don't know is whether I've had more than the average number of problems! I've had factory rifles with safeties that didn't work, floorplates that dropped open, iron sights that fell off, plus the normal litany of feeding, ejection, and extraction problems. And, believe it or not, I've seen the same kinds of problems with custom rifles.

Most of these problems were very easily fixed. Fortunately, I discovered most of them on the range, not in the field. Whether the firearm is new, used, or custom, you must start by inspecting it carefully. Check the bore. Check the stock for cracks. Check the bedding for obvious gaps or bearing surfaces. Check the sights—bent front sights aren't uncommon on used rifles! Check all the mechanical functions—and check feeding with a full magazine, not just a round in the chamber or one or two on top. Push-feed bolt-actions occasionally—perhaps even often—have too much or too little spring tension in the follower. They may feed perfectly with just one round in the magazine but fail to work at all with two or three. Controlled-round-feed bolt-actions, by the way, are not free from these problems.

I agree with Rich Reiley that such problems shouldn't exist. But it's not a perfect world, and they do exist. Shame on you if you don't discover the bugs—if any—before you take a rifle hunting!

Which leads to one last consideration. Whether the rifle you buy is new, used, semi-custom, or a full-up custom job, allow plenty of time to shoot it and get used to it before you head to the field. This has often been one of my greatest problems. Test guns never arrive on time, and I can't tell you how many times I have received, on the eve of a hunt, a rifle I planned to take and discovered a last-minute problem. Every time, I've sworn I would never do this again . . . but it's the nature of the business. Custom rifles, or brand-new models, will never be delivered early.

When you're shopping for a production rifle, new or used, at least you can dictate *when* you make the purchase. Don't wait until the week before hunting season. June and July are excellent gun-buying months. That gives you plenty of time—time you *need*—to get a scope mounted, check out the mechanical functioning several times, find the right load, and above all, get comfortable with your choice.

If you give yourself that kind of time, and spend it getting used to the rifle, working out any bugs you discover, and fitting the rifle to you and you to it, then it doesn't matter whether you choose to buy new, used, or custom. By the time the season rolls around it will be your rifle, and it will perform for you.

—————— ≡≡ CHAPTER SIX ≡≡ ——————

TAKING STOCK

Just thirty years ago, when I was starting to learn about rifles, the matter of gunstocks was a simple one. Gunstocks were wood, period. Generally speaking, they were walnut, although the occasional maple gunstock was seen, as were a few in more exotic hardwoods. Laminates existed, but as far as I knew they were for benchrest shooters; I never saw a laminated sporter stock until just a few years ago. If synthetic stocks existed at all, I never saw or heard of one.

Things have changed a lot. I don't know exactly when the first synthetic stocks came along, but like laminates, they got their start in target stocks. It seems to me that the first synthetic sporter stocks came along about twenty-five years ago, with then-radical gunsmiths like Gale McMillan and Chet Brown paving the way. Walnut remains the most common stock material in new factory rifles—although by a decreasing margin—but in the aftermarket "drop-in" stock business and in semi-custom and custom rifles, I am reasonably certain that synthetic stocks lead the way today. Most major manufacturers now offer synthetic stocks as a factory option as well. Laminated sporter stocks are much less common, but most major manufacturers also offer laminates as factory options, and there are plenty of custom and aftermarket laminates as well.

It's a myth that synthetic-stocked rifles are more accurate than wooden stocks. It depends on the barrel and the matching of the load to the rifle, just like everything else. It is true, however, that it's generally simpler and, for the maker, cheaper, to bed synthetic stocks.

The gunstock business today is not only much more diverse than it used to be, it's also gotten confusing. Let's start with several myths that have developed along with the other-than-walnut options. The first myth is that rifles stocked in synthetics and laminates shoot better than walnut-stocked rifles.

This is simply not true. Synthetic stocks *and* laminates are both more stable than wood, meaning they are less subject to warping during humidity changes. But they do not necessarily produce more accuracy.

The most accurate rifle I own is an 8mm Remington Magnum, built on a Remington Model 700 action by Rogue River Rifleworks and stocked in a very nice piece of English walnut. The most *consistent* rifle I own is a 7mm Remington Magnum built by David Miller. Miller's partner, Curt Crum, stocked it in a very nice piece of French walnut, and of course it's glass-bedded throughout. I've had the rifle for about twelve years now. Depending on which load I use and how I feel on a given day, it delivers groups ranging from just under a half-inch to just under an inch—rarely better, never worse. More importantly, in twelve years it has never shifted zero, even the slightest. I shoot bullets of 154 to 165 grains, and this is one of those "forgiving" rifles that seem to shoot virtually all loads in that bullet weight range to more or less the same point of impact. In twelve years I have never adjusted the scope. Yes, I have synthetic-stocked rifles that have also remained consistent— but you expect that with synthetics. Properly bedded wood will do just as well.

The stock is just one of many factors affecting accuracy. Actually, the stock itself has nothing to do with accuracy, but the way the action and barrel are *bedded* into the stock has a great deal to do with accuracy. It is not necessarily easier to bed a synthetic stock than a wooden stock, and a pure wooden stock and a laminate are the same in this regard. If a barrel and action are glass-bedded throughout, then even a solid wood stock should not shift under normal circumstances. Mind you, a week of solid rain or a few days at the bottom of a lake may cause enough swelling to make any wooden stock change impact, but under normal use, including the occasional rain shower, a fully glass-bedded wooden stock should not shift. However, this is the most time-consuming and most difficult way to bed a stock. A synthetic stock is absolutely impervious to moisture and a laminate nearly so. So long as it provides adequate accuracy, bedding can be a lot sloppier in those materials than with wood and it still will not shift.

The other great gunstock myth that seems in vogue today is that synthetic stocks are lighter than wood. On average this is true, but it is not always so. Wooden stocks vary tremendously in weight. Maple is lighter than walnut (but is just about as strong), and walnut varies tremendously in density and weight. A straight-grained, fairly plain piece of walnut is generally much lighter than a heavily figured stock. Synthetics also vary. Some synthetic stocks are made of solid material, and these are often just as heavy as wood. Other synthetic stocks are essentially just an outer shell, usually reinforced in the high-stress areas like the pistol grip but hollow through much of the butt. These synthetic stocks are indeed lighter than most wooden stocks, certainly wooden stocks of similar dimensions, but you cannot make a blanket statement that synthetics are lighter than wood.

Most laminate stocks are heavier than either wood or synthetic, especially the laminates that are resin-impregnated for added stability. This is also not universal. You can get a lot of weight off either wood or laminate by simply removing material. This benefit is not without trade-offs; in my opinion stock dimension and style have more to do with accentuating or attenuating felt recoil than anything else. Very slender stocks with thin combs and skimpy butts are much more likely to bruise your cheek and hurt your shoulder than more generous stocks with broad, rounded combs and wider, deeper butts.

It's also a good deal easier to modify the dimensions of a wooden stock than it is a synthetic. A synthetic stock is what it is, and about the only thing you can do to change its dimensions is shorten it. A wooden stock can be reshaped in many ways; you can shorten it, you can remove wood from a comb that's too high, you can reshape a pistol grip or fore-end. Although it's far more difficult and much beyond my skill level, I've seen many wooden stocks that were lengthened or had the comb raised by the skillful addition of another piece of wood. This is virtually impossible with a synthetic stock.

So what's best—wood, synthetic, or laminate? Actually, none of them are "best." I'm enough of an old-timer that I much prefer the warmth and beauty of nice wood. However, my hunting rifles are just about equally divided between walnut and synthetic. There is absolutely no question about which is more rugged— that goes to synthetics hands down. If you take a beautiful piece of walnut on a tough hunt in rugged country, it's going to get scratched up. If you take a walnut stock out in extremely wet country, there is always the risk of the stock warping and changing point of impact.

Minor scratches and dents are not the end of the world with even the fanciest wood. High-gloss stock finishes, like polyurethane and such, are very difficult to repair, but a bit of rubbing with linseed oil will conceal, if not erase, most minor

Laminated stocks are exceptionally rugged and stable, but tend to be heavier than solid wood. There are a number of sporters stocked in synthetics, but long-range rifles and varminters like this Ruger Model 77 are more common.

blemishes on oil-finished wood. A warm iron applied over a wet cloth will take care of even fairly major dents in a wooden stock. And when wood starts looking really bad, you can always completely refinish the stock and recut the checkering. However, synthetics also win in the maintenance department. The finish on most synthetic stocks is just paint.

I tend to think of synthetic stocks as functional but ugly, so I have never worried about scratches and blemishes on mine. But if you think of them as somehow attractive, or if you're a neatnik who can't abide a break in your camouflaged paint scheme, then touch-up paints are available—and when things get bad, you can simply have the stock repainted. A synthetic stock is also generally stronger than wood. It will not crack or split, and though I haven't tested the theory, I believe a synthetic stock is more likely to survive a catastrophe, like a horse rolling on it, than a wooden stock.

Laminated stocks are much more difficult to work than wood. Scratches and dents are harder to remove—but most laminates are also harder and tougher than solid wood, and it takes more abuse to ding them up. I must admit that I have relatively little experience with laminates, and have never owned a rifle so stocked. I have used a variety of laminated stocks for short periods, and my "take" on them is that they are stronger than solid wood, and perhaps stronger than most synthetics. They are certainly more

This Centennial edition of the famed Winchester Model 94 is a fine example of turn-of-the-century riflestocks. There is tremendous drop at heel; add that to the good-looking crescent buttplate and you've got lots of felt recoil—even from a mild-mannered .30-30.

The Monte Carlo comb was pioneered by Roy Weatherby but is offered by many makers today. This Steyr rifle has a stock very typical of the Monte Carlo design. It does tend to keep recoil away from the face, but the drop at heel tends to accentuate recoil to the shoulder.

stable than wood, though probably not as stable as synthetic. They will generally be the heaviest of the three.

Which you should choose depends mostly on where and how you hunt, but it also depends on you. If you really like good wood, then you'll probably not be happy with anything else. Take heart: most of the dings and scratches can be removed, and even if they can't, they become a part of the heritage of memories associated with a well-used hunting rifle. But if you do a lot of hunting on foot in rough country, or if you tend to get into a lot of snow and rain, synthetic is the way to go. If you can't handle the looks of synthetic, or if you're shooting a rifle with lots of recoil and you want gun weight, then a laminated stock makes a very sound option.

One thing to keep in mind: Most gunstocks are made with "Mr. Average" in mind. I'm about five feet eight inches in height with a medium build; I'm Mr. Average, and most factory gunstocks fit me just about right. If you're not Mr. Average— whether you're significantly taller or shorter, or have a longer or shorter neck or arms—then it's unlikely that a factory stock will fit you. Again, about the only thing you can do with a synthetic stock from the factory is make it shorter. You can order a custom synthetic with a longer length of pull, but there isn't much to be done about height of comb. If you need significantly different

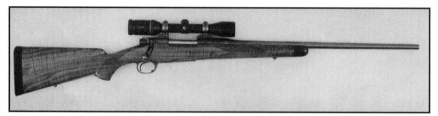

The Dakota Model 76 is a fine example of a semi-custom rifle sporting an American Classic stock style. The fore-end tip is pure cosmetics, but the good, thick recoil pad is a feature every riflestock should have.

stock dimensions than Mr. Average, a wooden stock is the most easily modified.

Since we seem to have found our way there, let's continue to discuss stock fit. Regardless of action, caliber, sights, and stock material, the object is for you to be able to raise the rifle to your shoulder in one fluid motion and have the sights come naturally into alignment with the target. Length of pull is the distance from trigger to butt. With your elbow crooked at ninety degrees and your trigger finger curled as if it were on the trigger, the proper length of pull for most people is the distance from the pad of your trigger finger to the inside of your elbow.

A stock that is too long will catch under your arm when you bring the rifle up, and a stock that is too short will generally kick hell out of you—and in either case it will be difficult for you to achieve rapid sight alignment. Note here that your "perfect" length of pull assumes you aren't wearing several layers of heavy clothes! This makes a big difference; the stock that is perfect in shirtsleeves will probably be a bit too long in the dead of winter. Since it's impractical to have "summer rifles" and "winter rifles," most of us settle on a compromise stock that's a quarter-inch to a half-inch *shorter* than our ideal dimensions, to prevent the butt from catching in heavy clothes.

Length of pull is the easiest stock dimension to alter. You can lengthen by using a thicker buttplate or recoil pad, and you can shorten by removing a small slice of the butt and resetting the pad. Unfortunately, *height of comb* is an equally critical dimension—perhaps more so in terms of both sight alignment and recoil attenuation—and is much more difficult to do something about.

Height of comb is generally measured in two ways—drop at comb and drop at heel, the comb being the portion of the stock behind the pistol grip, and the heel the uppermost portion of the butt. The drop is expressed as measurement below (or above) the centerline of the bore. To my mind, the ideal height of comb is whatever dimension enables you to raise the rifle to shoulder and cheek and have the sights—or scope—aligned with your eyes. You should not have to raise your head to see through the scope, nor should you have to scrunch your face down onto the stock to get a good sight picture. The sights should come into alignment naturally, with your head upright or slightly cocked forward, and with the stock firmly welded to the fleshiest part of your cheek.

There are two primary ways to achieve this. One is by having a stock that runs very straight from the beginning of the comb (the raised portion behind the pistol grip) to the heel. In other words, there is very little difference between drop-at-comb and drop-at-heel measurements. We have come to call this the "American Classic" stock style. The other common style, called the "Monte Carlo" comb, has a comb that slants upward from the pistol grip, then drops down sharply to the heel. This type of stock was popularized in rifles by Roy Weatherby, and his Monte Carlo comb remains a characteristic feature of the Weatherby Mark V.

These two basic styles—American Classic with a straight comb, and the Monte Carlo with the raised comb and dropped heel—are the most common riflestock styles today. It took a long time to get to this point. No one seems to know why, but from the early days of the Pennsylvania rifle, through the nineteenth century, and well into this century, American riflestocks were made with vast amounts of drop. Shoulder a vintage Winchester lever-action, a classic Remington rolling-block, or a turn-of-the-century Savage

99, and try to see the sights without raising your head. Most of us can't do it. Then imagine the machinations required if such rifles wore scopes instead of iron sights!

Too much drop remained a standard evil in American riflestocks until quite recently. Roy Weatherby was among the first to allow shooters to see properly through a scope—without raising the head—with his Monte Carlo comb. Although Weatherby's Monte Carlo has remained one of the most radical, the Monte Carlo comb has become fairly standard with several major manufacturers. Bill Ruger took stock design a giant step forward when he hired custom gunmaker Lenard Brownell to design the stock for his Ruger Number One. The result was one of the straightest stocks ever put on an American factory rifle, and he echoed this straight-combed American Classic style when he brought out the Model 77 bolt-action.

Too much drop not only makes it more difficult to quickly attain a proper sight picture—especially with a scope—but also radically accentuates felt recoil. Recoil moves the rifle not only back into your shoulder but also up into your face. Recoil is natural and you can't stop it, but since your cheek is more tender than your shoulder, you want to direct as much force as possible into your shoulder and as little as possible into your face. The more drop to the stock, the more upward recoil. For example, one of the hardest-kicking factory rifles ever made was almost certainly the Winchester Model 1895 in .405 Winchester. The standard stock had an incredible amount of drop (and a skinny little crescent buttplate, which we'll talk about later), and it was absolutely brutal to shoot.

As Jim Carmichel aptly points out in his master work, *Book of the Rifle*, the Monte Carlo comb doesn't really cure this problem. The raised comb does allow a proper and natural sight picture, but the drop down to the heel does cause more recoil to the face. This is indeed mitigated somewhat by the slanted comb sliding away from the face, but I believe the best stock design

Perfect stock fit is elusive in that there is no way that a rifle can fit perfectly in shirtsleeves and still fit when you're wearing this much clothing! If you do your rangework in warm weather but do most of your hunting in the cold, you might be better off with a slightly short buttstock.

for recoil attenuation is one that runs very straight from comb to heel. This places the butt high on the shoulder and keeps recoil coming straight back about as much as is possible.

Now, the height of comb that is correct for you depends on your facial build and the height of your sights. If you are using iron sights, then the proper height of comb is much lower than it will be if you are using a powerful scope that requires "high" scope rings. This is the real fallacy of both detachable scopes with auxiliary iron sights and the "see-through" scope mounts that used to be fairly popular. It is impossible to have a stock that is ideal for both iron sights and for use with a scope, the centerline of which may be as much as an inch higher than the irons.

This does not mean that a detachable scope with iron sights is necessarily a bad idea, but you should decide which is the *primary* sight, and this is the sight that should come up properly aligned when you raise the rifle. For most North American hunting today, this will be the scope—and this is the way most American factory rifles are stocked. For instance, I just grabbed the used Remington 700 ADL and threw it to my shoulder. This rifle has a wooden stock with a Monte Carlo comb. It has iron sights, but with the rifle properly cheeked I'm actually looking *above* the sights. This rifle is stocked for scope use, and only by consciously scrunching my face down into the stock can I obtain a sight picture with the iron sights.

That's perfectly fine. We will mount a scope on this rifle, and the iron sights will serve purely as backup. I have two other rifles that are good illustrations of this height-of-comb dilemma. One is a Winchester Model 70 .375, made sometime after World War II. The other is a John Rigby .416. The Model 70 has a mild Monte Carlo comb that is ideal for use with a low-mounted, low-power scope, which is perfect for a .375. I have Talley detachable mounts on the rifle, and in a pinch I can use the irons—but to do so I have to consciously scrunch my face into the stock to get a sight picture. The Rigby .416 has a straight classic-style stock, and it also wears a low-power scope in detachable mounts. But this one is set up to be perfect for use with iron sights on the theory that, should I use it to hunt buffalo or elephant in very thick cover, I will probably remove the scope. I can easily get a good sight picture through the scope—but I have to consciously keep my head a bit straighter than I normally do.

If a comb is too high, the problem is easily fixed by removing a bit of stock material. Unfortunately, especially with the current trend toward more powerful scopes and larger objectives that must be mounted ever higher, it is more common for a comb to be too low. This is harder to fix. A new stock with a higher comb is probably the best answer, but there are strap-on cheekpieces available, and if you don't mind the aesthetics, you can actually build up a comb—especially on synthetic stocks—with plastic wood. The main thing to keep

One of the stock rooms at Bishop's Gunstocks in Warsaw, Missouri, where I spent much of my misspent youth. If stock fit is a problem, replacement stocks from firms like Bishop's and Fajen's, also in Warsaw, are an available and inexpensive solution.

in mind is that the rifle simply must come up naturally with the primary sights in alignment.

Whether you want a cheekpiece or not depends largely on your tastes and, to a much lesser degree, your facial build. I actually prefer the clean lines of a buttstock without a cheekpiece, and if the comb is gently rounded I see no real utility in one. But a shooter with a long, thin face may feel altogether different. If you're starting from scratch, you should go to a well-stocked gunshop and heft as wide a variety of gunstocks as you can to see what works for you.

There are other stock styles, of course. The thumbhole stock keeps popping up now and again, and it has advantages. A thumbhole can be made even straighter than a traditional pistol grip stock and so is probably the very best in attenuating recoil. Because of the very secure grip, it also directs some amount of recoil into the shooting hand, which also helps. I don't like thumbholes, purely from a looks standpoint, but the only drawback they have is that, should you need to shoot fast, they're a bit slower to get into action unless your shooting hand is already in place.

A quick word about full-length "Mannlicher-style" stocks is in order. I like their looks very much, but that's all there is to them: looks. There is no advantage to a full-length stock, and there are very real disadvantages. They add absolutely unnecessary gun weight, plus they are the very devil to bed properly and get to shoot. Having said that, I do love the way they look!

I think a hunting rifle's stock should be checkered, whether it's synthetic, wood, or laminate. This is not purely looks; in wet or hot weather, when your hands are damp or sweaty, checkering helps you get a good grip, and can be important in fast-breaking situations. This is a potential drawback to laminates. They can be checkered, but it's the very devil to do. Impressed checkering patterns have gotten very good in synthetic stocks, but the rough "crinkle paint" finish is almost as good. A drawback to this textured paint is that I've had it take the skin right off my cheek! A bit of fine sandpaper applied to the comb and cheekpiece helps.

Pistol grip caps and fore-end tips are purely cosmetic, as are whatever spacers—white, black, pink, you name it—that go between the fore-end tip, pistol grip cap, buttplate, and the stock. But whatever goes on the butt is not. The good old crescent buttplate that started in the days of the Pennsylvania rifle and continued in vogue until early in this century is a disaster. What you want is a straight or *very slightly* curved buttplate more or less perpendicular to the line of sight. Like most of us, I admire the looks of a checkered steel buttplate—but the only way to go is a rubber recoil pad. On light-recoiling rifles, a thin rifle pad is fine, but on heavier rifles you want a good, thick pad. Better, get a good thick pad made of one of the shock-absorbing polymers like Pachmayr's Decelerator. Aside from recoil attenuation, only a recoil pad offers the nonslip surface that you want.

Aside from what kind of pad you put on it, the depth and width of the butt also make a huge difference in felt recoil. The more surface area you can spread the recoil over, the less you will feel it. Of course, a very big butt is unsightly (no pun intended; I just don't know how else to say it!), but just ¼ inch in every direction creates a lot more surface area and will make a big difference in felt recoil. A good example is the stock on the good old Winchester Model 94. Today's stock doesn't have as much drop as did stocks of a century ago, but it's very slim and trim— and it makes the very mild .30-30 cartridge kick a whole lot more than it should.

The last feature of a hunting rifle stock that should be mentioned is sling swivel studs. Given a choice, I much prefer the two-screw varieties, but Uncle Mike's round, detachable sling swivel studs are more or less universal. That's what most of my rifles wear, and they're fine. However, on heavy-recoiling rifles, that round stud will bite into your hand. On big rifles, I absolutely believe in a barrel-mounted forward swivel. The barrel-mounted swivel also has the advantage of putting the slung rifle lower on the shoulder, making it easier to go through brush. Many of us prefer its looks, so why not go for a nice barrel-band swivel on all hunting rifles?

There is a price. If you shoot with a tight sling, a barrel-mounted sling swivel will put tension on the barrel and change the relationship between barrel and bedding. Rifles with barrel-mounted swivels will usually shoot to a different point of impact with a tight sling than if shot without the sling. This is normally not enough to matter on a dangerous-game rifle but can make a big difference on a general-purpose hunting rifle.

The hunting rifle stock is more than just a handle. How well it is mated to the action and barrel is critical to accuracy. Its design, more than anything else, dictates how much or how little you feel recoil. Most important of all, whether or not it fits you determines how well and how quickly you are able to get your shot off when the trophy of a lifetime appears. Most existing stocks can be readily modified to correct any ills. However, replacement stocks, whether wood, synthetic, or laminate, are incredibly cheap today. For comfortable, accurate shooting there is simply no substitute for a proper stock that fits you.

CHAPTER SEVEN

THE LONG AND SHORT OF BARRELS

The barrel is a rifle's soul. As is the case with people, what's inside is far more important than what's on the outside. A barrel can be short or long, thick or thin; how well it shoots depends mostly on its inner qualities. As is also the case with people, the inside is something you can do very little about. Fortunately most barrels, like most people, are pretty good. Some are great, but a few are just plain rotten.

There are several things that can make a good barrel shoot bad. The action or barrel can be poorly bedded, causing shifting or pressure that will throw shots wild. Poor accuracy can be as simple as ammo that the rifle doesn't like, or loose action screws or a shifting scope mount. It can even be as simple as fouling. We'll cover all these subjects in subsequent chapters, but I want to say this here: Not all barrels are created equal, and once in a while you run into a bad barrel. You can put it through all kinds of rehab, you can re-bed it several different ways, and you can send it off to be microscopically smoothed and cryogenically relieved. You may even improve it some. But you will still have a bad barrel. If the cheap fixes don't work, I can't recommend spending money on exotic spas for barrels. A bad barrel is a bad barrel, and the best thing to do is replace it quickly!

As with stocks, there are several myths surrounding barrels. The most prevalent legend is that stiff, heavy barrels shoot better than pencil-thin barrels. This is simply not true. All things being equal, it is easier to make a heavy-barreled rifle shoot well, primarily because a heavy barrel vibrates less while the bullet is traveling down it. This makes bedding much less critical. But a light barrel of good quality is capable of the same accuracy as a heavy barrel of like quality. The big difference is that light barrels heat up quicker. As metal heats, it expands. When the metal of a barrel expands, the vibrations change and the bullets start to "walk"—usually upward on the target. A heavy barrel heats slower and so will normally allow more shots to be fired sequentially before barrel heat opens the group.

This is extremely important in target and varmint rifles, but is not significant in hunting rifles. Even a very slender barrel is normally capable of three-shot groups, and this is more shots than you need in at least 99 percent of all hunting situations. If you have a light-barreled rifle and you want to find out how it really shoots, get all set up on the bench and fire one shot. Then walk away and let the barrel cool completely, waiting at least five minutes—ten in warm weather. When you go back to the bench, make absolutely certain the rifle is in the same position—the fore-end is in the same spot on the sandbags, the butt is snugged the same. Then fire another shot and repeat the cooling. It's amazing how well light barrels really can shoot when you give them time!

Another misconception about barrels is that longer ones shoot better than short barrels. Simply not true. In fact, it may well be the opposite. Given equal exterior dimensions and like caliber, short barrels are "stiffer" and vibrate less than longer barrels, which, again, makes bedding less critical. The short, thick barrels put on bolt-action pistols, for instance, are often capable of spectacular accuracy.

However, it's the quality of the rifling that enables a barrel to shoot well. There are several barrel-making techniques. Button-rifling is created by pulling a "button" through a drilled blank,

Specialty pistols like the XP-100 blow holes in the myth that short barrels aren't as accurate as long barrels. All things being equal, barrels that are short and stiff tend to be exceptionally accurate.

cutting the grooves. This is generally the least expensive barrel-making technique. Hammer-forging is done by using massive pressure to pound the barrel around a mandril. The equipment required is fabulously expensive, so only a few large manufacturers make barrels by this technique. Then there's good old cut or "broached" rifling, the original technique, in which the rifling is actually cut into the barrel. Manufacturers will argue convincingly that their barrels, made by one of these techniques, are the best. They're neither right nor wrong; good barrels can be made by any of these techniques. The trick is to make them *well*, regardless of how they are made.

No two rifle barrels are exactly alike. Some are a few ten-thousandths undersized and some are a bit oversized. Some are dead straight and some are not. Some are fairly rough while others are very smooth. The perfect barrel probably has yet to be made, but subtle, almost microscopic differences separate great barrels from good barrels . . . and allow a very few bad barrels to slip through.

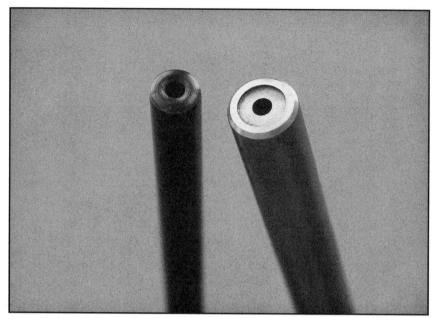

The muzzle is the last thing that touches the bullet, so the last part of the rifling is critical to accuracy. On the left is a standard "rounded" crown; on the right a recessed or "target" crown. The method doesn't matter, but the crown must be absolutely square.

Major manufacturers have a tremendous advantage. Some make their own barrels and thus can run their own quality control. Others source their barrels, specifying the level of quality, but by buying hundreds or thousands of them, they're able to get decent barrels much more cheaply than you or I can. Either way, factory barrels are pretty good and generally very consistent, but there are limits. In the rare case where you get a truly bad barrel, you can get another one of like quality (or the quality the original should have been) installed for maybe $150 or so, much less than the cost of a new rifle. The manufacturer (whether he made it or purchased it) probably wouldn't have fifty bucks in a similar barrel. Now, if you're a serious accuracy nut, you may invest in a match-grade barrel. You could pay $500 or more for the rifled barrel— before chambering and crowning. Sometimes a factory barrel, or an over-the-counter replacement barrel, will deliver half-inch groups. A match-grade barrel, if well chambered and bedded, can be expected to deliver at least this level of accuracy—and will often cut it in half. With the possible exception of serious long-range rifles, you don't need that level of accuracy in a hunting rifle. But here's the point: You should not expect that you're getting a $500 barrel in a sporting rifle that costs within a few hundred bucks of that figure!

That said, the barrels coming out of the factories are darned good, and out-of-the-box accuracy is better than ever. If you've tried everything and you're still getting 2-inch groups from a bolt-action rifle, you could well have a bad barrel . . . but it's rare.

There are many types of rifling. The number of lands and grooves vary from 2 (in mass-produced World War II barrels) to 8, with 6 the most common—and then there's Marlin's Micro-Groove barrel, with numerous small lands and grooves. There's polygonal rifling and "gain twist" rifling. Again, how well the barrel is made is the most important factor.

The rate of twist *is* important. Several hundred years ago it was discovered that imparting a spin to a projectile stabilized it in flight and greatly increased accuracy. There is such a thing as too much spin—overstabilization—and too little spin—understabilization. The round balls in use when rifling was created require very little spin for stabilization; muzzleloaders designed to fire round balls have a very slow twist, with one revolution in 48 inches of barrel common. Now, the longer the projectile the faster it must spin to stabilize. Depending on caliber and the associated common bullet weights, most sporting rifles today have barrel twists ranging from one turn in 8 inches to one turn in 12 inches.

Most general-purpose .30-caliber sporting rifles (.30-06, .308, .300 magnum) are barreled with rifling of one turn in 10 inches. In most calibers the "window of stabilization" is not all that narrow, and it isn't in the .30s. Rifling of one turn in 10 inches is probably optimum for bullets of 165 to 180 grains, but it will provide good stabilization and accuracy with bullets of

150 to 200 grains in most rifles. No two barrels are exactly alike, but if you want the best accuracy with 220-grain bullets, you may need a slightly faster twist. You will almost certainly want a faster twist if you want to shoot an ultra-heavyweight like Sierra's 240-grain, .30-caliber match bullet. Similarly, your 1-in-10 twist will probably overstabilize the short, light-for-caliber 110-grain, .30-caliber "varmint" bullet.

You usually don't need to worry about all of this. The manufacturers barrel their rifles to be suitable for the widest possible range of common bullet weights. You need to be concerned about it if you're dead set on using an extra-heavy or extra-light bullet, or if you are rebarreling a rifle. Another time it's worth worrying about is when you're getting erratic accuracy from a rifle of unknown origin. Just maybe the previous owner had odd tastes in bullet weights! If you want to know what twist your rifle has, it's simple. Just make a mark on a cleaning rod about twenty inches back from the end of the jag. Put enough patch on the rod to "take" the rifling, and push it into the bore from the muzzle. When your mark has made one full revolution, stop and make another mark on the cleaning rod at the muzzle. Pull it out and measure the distance from your second mark to the end of the jag. That distance should be the twist of your rifling.

Except in rare circumstances, you can generally take as a given that your barrel has a rifling twist that will suffice for the bullet weights you are most likely to use. It's much more common to have problems with either end of the barrel. The aft end of the barrel has several portions, all of which must be cut with precision. The *chamber* is, of course, the unrifled portion of the barrel that is reamed to fit the designated cartridge. Once in a while you run into a sloppy chamber. The most obvious symptom is short case life, but poor accuracy can surely result. Even more critical to performance, if not necessarily to accuracy, is the *throat*—the unrifled portion between the chamber and the *leade*, or the beginning of the rifling.

The throat length controls the seating depth of your bullet, which in turn impacts powder capacity. This is not particularly important to shooters of factory ammo, but is extremely important to handloaders. It is often desirable to seat the bullets a bit farther out than factory specs call for, thus increasing powder capacity and enabling a bit more velocity. The .257 Roberts is a good example of a cartridge that benefits tremendously from a longer-than-normal throat. Weatherby has traditionally gone a step farther, incorporating *freebore* into its factory rifles. Freebore is a short section of unrifled barrel ahead of the chamber, longer than is necessary for any throat. This smoothbore section delays the inevitable pressure spike when the bullet slams into the rifling, and is one of the factors that allow Weatherby to load its factory ammo to higher velocities and pressures than other manufacturers. Freebore, by the way, is generally not the best route to accuracy. Most often, the highest level of accuracy is obtained when the bullet is seated so that it's just a few thousandths off the lands.

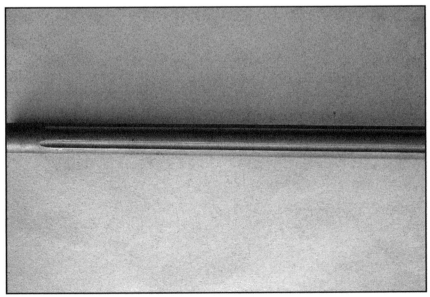

Fluting is seen more and more frequently on hunting rifles. It reduces weight without reducing strength, and also allows the barrel to cool more quickly.

The *crown* is the dressed end of the rifling at the muzzle. Most often the crown is gently rounded in sporting rifles, but it may be recessed. The exact form doesn't matter, but the crown must be skillfully done and must be at a consistent right angle to the bore. The last thing the bullet touches when it leaves the barrel is the end of the rifling. There can be terrible pits and gouges throughout the bore. The chamber can be out-of-round, and the throat can be eroded. Even with these problems a barrel can shoot surprisingly well—but if the crown isn't square or if there's a problem with the rifling at the muzzle, good accuracy is very unlikely. By the way, a crown can easily be recut, often requiring a short section of barrel to be lopped off. This is a frequent solution for accuracy problems, especially in rifles that have been cleaned from the muzzle over extended periods.

Most of the nuances of the barrel's interior will be decided for you, and are based on standard dimensions that are appropriate for standard cartridges and bullets. The primary choice you will

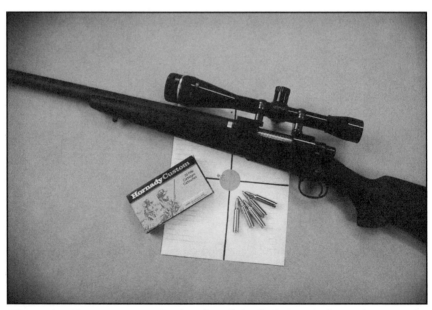

This is the Christensen Arms "carbon-barreled rifle." It isn't the synthetic coating that gives this .22-250 its accuracy; Christensen starts with very good barrels.

usually have to make is barrel length. Though it is not true that short barrels are less accurate than long barrels, it is absolutely true that short barrels don't generate as much velocity as long barrels. Unfortunately, there is no exact formula that can tell you just how much faster a barrel of, say, 24 inches will be compared to a barrel of 20 inches. It depends on the cartridge, the propellant powder used, and also on the individual barrel. Again, no two barrels are alike. A barrel that is slightly tighter will generate more pressure per grain of propellant—and more velocity. It is therefore quite possible that a "tight" 20-inch barrel will generate more velocity than a "loose" 24-inch barrel of like caliber. On the other hand, if that same "tight" barrel was also 24 inches, it would be even faster.

As a general rule of thumb, you can expect to lose somewhere between 25 and 35 feet per second per inch as you drop from about 24 inches to 20 inches. Large-cased magnum cartridges tend to lose more velocity than standard cartridges, and at some point below 20 inches the rate of loss will increase. This is not very definitive information, but there are so many variables that it's hard to be more exact. In real terms, however, the loss of 100 or even 150 feet per second is not significant over normal game ranges.

Even so, I don't personally care for extremely short barrels— but it depends on what you're using the rifle for. On belted magnums or rifles intended for use in open country, I want a minimum of a 24-inch barrel, and I have several 26-inch barrels among my hunting rifles. The longer barrel does indeed wring out a bit more velocity, and in open country you may as well have all you can get. I also like the weight up forward that you get with a longer barrel; for me it makes the rifle handle better and hold more steadily. Longer barrels, especially those of 26 inches and beyond, also have noticeably less muzzle blast than short barrels, especially with very fast cartridges.

On the other hand, there's such a thing as too much of a good thing. On a couple of occasions I've taken a 26-inch-barreled bolt-action into a whitetail stand and found that long barrel to be extremely awkward in close quarters. A 24-inch barrel makes a good compromise, and the standard 22-inch barrel remains a very good length for non-magnum hunting cartridges. If you happen

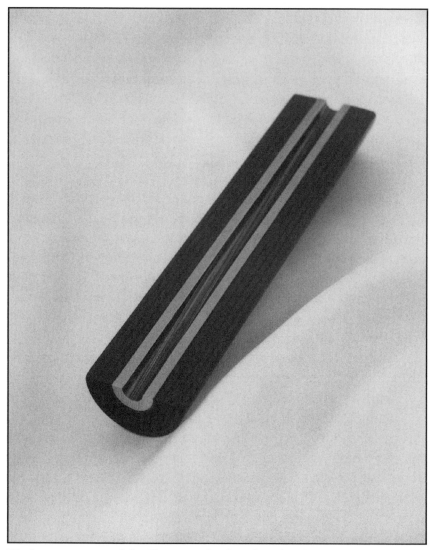

Here's a cross-section of the Christensen "carbon" barrel. The interior is a good steel barrel, turned pencil-thin and reinforced with a graphite casing. The effect is the stiffness and stability of a bull barrel with the weight of a sporter barrel.

to like shorter barrels, you really aren't losing much—but I'm not sure you're gaining a whole lot in handiness, either.

Another decision you can make involves exterior dimensions. Few specifications of sporting rifles are offered in differing barrel contours, but these days most companies offer lightweight models as well as standard-weight sporters. The lightweight version will probably wear a synthetic stock, but you can almost bet that it will have a thinner, lighter barrel. Stock materials make a difference, but steel is heavier than wood *or* fiberglass. The fastest way to take weight off a rifle is to reduce barrel steel. This is not bad. As we've seen, thin barrels aren't necessarily less accurate. My Match Grade Arms .300 Winchester Magnum weighs just over six pounds *with scope*. The barrel is a wee, pencil-like affair—but the rifle will hold three shots inside of $3/8$ inch.

My problem with thin barrels is that I find them whippy and hard to control, especially if I'm out of breath or excited. A lightweight rifle with a lightweight barrel definitely has a place. But for ease of shooting I much prefer a fairly stiff barrel that puts plenty of weight up forward. The stiffer barrel is easier to bed, and it's also easier to find out how well it shoots. Very light barrels are time-consuming on the range because you're always waiting for them to cool!

The two "project" Model 700s I've acquired for subsequent chapters both have 22-inch barrels of medium contour. Since the caliber is .30-06, I think the length is about right, and the profile is also about right. However, on a hunting rifle both length and contour have much more to do with personal taste than performance. A good barrel will shoot well if it's bedded right and fed good ammo, regardless of its diameter or length.

These days you see more and more factory rifles offered with fluted barrels. Fluting has nothing to do with performance, but it is a good way to reduce weight without reducing stiffness, and the flutes also aid in heat dissipation. This last is far more important in varmint and target rifles than big-game rifles.

Another subject worth touching on is barrel materials. These days most barrels are either good old chrome-moly or stainless steel, but an increasing number of titanium barrels is also available. It is my sense that the most accurate barrels are still chrome-moly, followed by stainless, with titanium in third place. In terms of barrel life, you can reverse that order. Stainless has pretty well come of age, and titanium is coming on fast. Stainless steel has a significant advantage in wet or salt air coastal climates. Titanium is not only rustproof but also tougher than steel and much lighter in weight. It is more expensive and much more difficult to work with, and only a few custom makers are messing with it, but I expect we'll see much more of it in years to come. The main thing to remember is that, just like the method with which the rifling is cut, the quality of the work is more important than the material. I should also mention the "carbon barrels" being produced by Christensen Arms. This is actually a misnomer. The Christensen barrel is very much a steel barrel, except that the craftsmen take a steel barrel and turn it down to a pencil and *reinforce* it with graphite. The result is great strength and wonderful heat dissipation with very little weight. It works, but it's not really a synthetic barrel.

At the beginning I referred to some techniques for "barrel rehabilitation." There are a number of barrel coatings and treatments, and these are increasing all the time. The two that I am most familiar with and that are most popular at this writing are Blackstar Barrel Accurizing and cryogenic relieving. These are not mutually exclusive; a barrel can be given both treatments, and neither is very expensive. Any gunsmith worth his salt can almost certainly give you current information on these and other processes to make your barrel better. But remember this: Nothing, but nothing, can make a silk purse out of a sow's ear. There is no cure for a bad barrel except a new barrel. There's also a corollary: Don't mess with success! Most of these treatments have a tendency to increase accuracy by some margin, but if you have a super-accurate barrel, love it and leave it alone!

I'm set up for a Montana whitetail with a Christensen Carbon Cannon in .300 Weatherby Magnum. This rifle was quite accurate, but no more so than a good .300 with a conventional barrel.

Blackstar Barrel Accurizing is a technique for microscopically "smoothing" the steel molecules of your barrel. Sometimes it radically improves accuracy, but once in a while it makes it worse. Normally it will take a good barrel and make it shoot a bit better. Sometimes it increases velocity, but usually not. What it will almost always do is reduce a barrel's tendency to foul. This can be important, especially if you have a "rough" bore that seems to foul very quickly. It can be worth pursuing, but it is not a cure for a hopeless barrel.

Cryogenic relieving is a process whereby a barrel is "deep-frozen" at several hundred degrees below zero, then thawed—both under controlled conditions. The freezing toughens and sort of "aligns" the molecules. "Cryo" may or may not improve accuracy. It may or may not reduce fouling (though it usually does). What it almost invariably does is extend barrel life—*significantly*. Although very inexpensive, it is probably not worth pursuing in a standard-caliber hunting rifle. It is definitely worth the effort in a varmint rifle or in a hot magnum with limited barrel life.

Just what is the life of a normal barrel? What's a "normal barrel?" Every barrel is different, and there is no rule of thumb. A .30-06 should be good for several thousand rounds. A .30-.378 or 7mm STW may start to lose accuracy long before you reach a thousand rounds. Most of us will never shoot a barrel out, but since every barrel is different it's almost impossible to say when "burnout" will occur. You can generally see the rifling in the throat start to fade first, but this may have no noticeable effect on accuracy for many more hundreds of rounds. Barrel life is not something you should worry about, except on used guns of uncertain background. Then, as I mentioned, factor in the potential cost of a new barrel. But if you start out with a new rifle, you can figure that you'll get your money's worth out of the barrel long before it gives up on you!

═══ CHAPTER EIGHT ═══

THE RIGHT SIGHT

The telescopic sight is pretty much universal today, and that's as it should be. Excepting a very few limited applications, the scope sight is superior to any and all iron sights. Let's quickly review why this is so.

There are three basic types of rifle sights: open sights, consisting of a front sight close to the muzzle and a rear sight normally mounted somewhere along the first third of the barrel; aperture sights, consisting of a similar front sight and a rear aperture in which the eye centers the tip of the front sight; and a scope sight. Open sights require the eye to focus in three planes: on the rear sight, the front sight, and the target. It is impossible for the eye to do this, so you have to go back and forth between the three. This is easier when you're young and becomes more difficult with age. Ultimately, the rear sight will stay blurry.

With the aperture or "peep" sight, you look *through* the rear aperture, not *at* it, so the problem is reduced to two focal planes instead of three. The eye naturally centers the bead or the tip of the rear sight in the center of the aperture, so, with practice, the peep sight is very fast and very efficient.

The telescopic sight reduces the eye's work to just one focal plane at the target. All you have to do is focus on the target and superimpose the reticle. This is the great advantage of the telescopic sight, but not the only one.

Optics have the ability to gather light. Both iron sights and peep sights become very hard to see as light dims, but a scope actually enhances your ability to see game in poor light. This is the second great advantage of the scope sight. The third and least important advantage is its ability to magnify the target. If you see it better, you can place your shot better. However, not all scopelike sights actually have magnification. There are "zero magnification" scopes for use on shotguns, and there are scopelike optical sights like the Aimpoint and Bushnell's hologram sight. Though these do not magnify, they do enhance low-light capabilities and allow aiming in just one focal plane—thus maintaining the two most important advantages of the scope sight.

For most hunting purposes, there should be no argument regarding which is the best sight. It's a scope, hands down, and it should be a traditional telescopic sight with some degree of

This Marlin .45-70, extensively remodeled by Idaho gunsmith Jim Brockman, featured a very clever "pop-up" peep sight. For close-range work the peep sight is every bit as good as a scope, and much better in rain or snow.

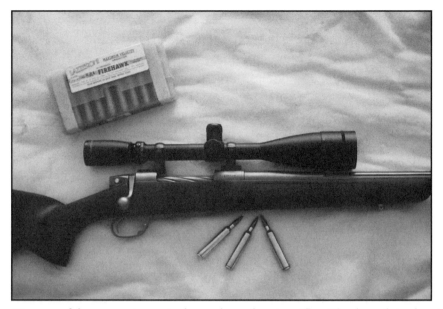

Big, powerful scopes are increasingly popular on hunting rifles. They have their place on specialized long-range rigs like this Lazzeroni, but they are cumbersome, overpowered, and downright impractical for most hunting situations.

magnification. How much depends on the country and the game, much like caliber selection. We'll talk about that later. First, let's look at some very specific hunting situations in which, despite all the foregoing, iron sights remain superior.

Many, perhaps even most, hunters consider iron sights to be faster than scopes, thus irons are often chosen for those elusive "brush rifles" and also for use on dangerous game. Regardless of what sight you choose, you must practice with it. Given practice, iron sights are not faster than scopes. We're talking fractions of seconds here, but it is *faster* for the eye to aim with a scope sight than with iron sights. Peep sights, especially those with a large aperture, are faster than traditional open sights, but neither is as fast as a scope. So I don't accept the argument that iron sights are the best choice for either brush rifles or for *most* hunting of dangerous game. A brush rifle for deer and bear and such should have a low-power scope. A rifle intended for use on lion or leopard should have a low-power scope—especially since the cats are most often taken at first or last light. In my experience, and I have a lot of it, a low-power scope can make a big difference when you're trying to sort a Cape buffalo bull from a herd—black animal in dark shadows. You can, however, hunt Cape buffalo very effectively with an open-sight rifle. If you're hunting elephant, then the scope doesn't matter at all; the target is huge, you will almost certainly be very close, and to get close you'll have to work your way through thornbush and tangled vines. The extra projection of a scope is just something more to get tangled up.

This last point is one of the significant disadvantages to a scope. It does create additional projections on the rifle, and if you have to crawl through seriously thick stuff, the cleaner profile of an open-sight rifle can make a difference. Under most circumstances the advantages of a scope, once you get through the thick stuff and are getting ready for a shot, are so valuable that it's worth dragging it along. But I've been in a couple of spots where a scope was just excess baggage.

Few of us have serious concerns about the right rifle for hunting elephant or following up Cape buffalo, but there are a couple of more common applications where iron sights remain superior to scopes. One of them is in rain or driving snow. Precipitation is the chief enemy of sights with lenses. You can protect them with lens caps, and you should, but if it's raining or snowing hard enough you still run the risk of being unable to see through your scope at a critical moment. Aperture sights are also not weatherproof; moisture has a habit of collecting in the aperture itself, making the sight useless until it's cleared. Even in a downpour you can usually find a way to protect your scope enough so you can use it, but open sights are the most reliable in very wet weather. Another good reason to have iron sights is in the rain forest whilst hunting dangerous game. The vegetation is so dense in certain areas that the distance between you and the game can be measured in a few feet. Here iron sights can save you valuable fractions of a second in dangerous situations.

Yet another application in which iron sights are superior is hound hunting, for bear or boar or whatever. Even if you shoot a scope with both eyes open, as you properly should, the scope sight has the effect of giving you "tunnel vision." With hound hunting you must be conscious of where the dogs are as you prepare to take your shot, and this is very difficult to do through a telescopic sight. Many serious houndsmen simply don't allow the use of scope sights, and I don't blame them.

Other than these very limited applications, I simply can't think of any other situations in which a scope is not superior. Generations ago the general belief was that scopes were unreliable and not nearly so rugged as iron sights. This was probably true in granddad's day, but although this myth persists, it is not true today. A well-made rear sight, especially a very simple sight like a standing express rear on a quarter rib or sturdy steel base, is nearly indestructible—but front sights tend to be fairly fragile and exposed. I have often seen them bent slightly to one side or the

I like a scope to be scaled to the rifle and caliber. This short-tubed Leupold 1.5-6X is ideal on a rifle like this Harris Gunworks short-action .308 Winchester.

other. And although the rear sight I have described is very sturdy, how many modern manufacturers actually supply such sights?

Iron sights as supplied by modern manufacturers are mostly a joke, and not a good one. They tend to be flimsy affairs, often plastic, with a folding blade that is relatively easy to knock off. Worse, factory rear sights are often very poorly attached to the barrel. I have had quite a number of rear sights—and a couple of front sights—actually fall off a rifle during the course of a tough hunt. Most of the time I was relying on a scope sight, so it didn't matter. But I had a rear sight, the *only* sight, fall off a .460 Weatherby Magnum in Africa once, and just last year I had a rear sight fall off an in-line muzzleloader. There may be reasons for using open sights, but do not take for granted that an iron sight, especially one supplied by the factory, is automatically foolproof.

I actually much prefer aperture sights to open sights. They're faster and allow much more precise aiming. Despite their superiority, I don't much care for the looks of scopes on traditional tubular-magazine lever-actions, so mine wear peep sights. However, the peep is also not the sturdiest of sights. They can bend or break, and when I'm using a rifle with this type of sighting equipment I try to be very careful with it.

The most rugged of sights is probably a well-mounted express rear with a single standing leaf. I won't argue that. But I honestly believe that a well-mounted scope is at worst the second most reliable type of sighting equipment. Scopes can fail, just like any other mechanical device, but it's rare. Modern scopes are dependable tools that can take incredible knocks and remain in zero. I trust them. I trust my pickup truck, too, but I carry an AAA card just in case.

If you're hunting close to home it's no big deal, but if you've traveled some distance to hunt you should have some kind of automotive assistance card in case of a failure. I submit that the very best backup system is a spare rifle. The scope can go or the rear sight can fall off, that's true, but it's far more likely for the stock to break, and some obscure mechanical malady is also

One oft-overlooked item in scope selection is eye relief. The more recoil you have, the more eye relief you need. If you don't have enough, sooner or later your scope will cut you.

possible. The best way to cover all the bases is to have a spare rifle with a scope, all sighted in and ready to go. It is not essential that everybody in camp have one. Few of us go hunting alone, and one spare rifle among a hunting party is always a good idea. Over the years I've had several rifles—either mine or my partner's—go belly up on a hunt. The problems have ranged from bizarre to mundane, but a scope has not been among them.

Even so, concern over a scope giving out in mid-hunt persists. Other than a spare rifle, there are really two ways to handle it. You can carry a spare scope, or you can rely on iron sights as a backup system. Personally, I don't worry about it too much. My dangerous-game rifles have iron sights, but most of my general-purpose rifles do not. If I'm going hunting alone on a long-range trip and I'm taking just one rifle, I usually do carry a spare scope set in rings, but I have never needed to use it. We'll talk about scope mounts in greater detail in the next chapter,

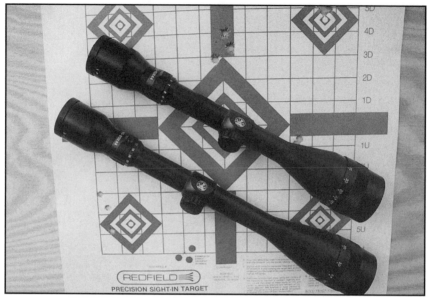

You get what you pay for in optics, but so long as you stick with reliable, recognizable brands you'll get your money's worth. These are two new scopes offered under Cabela's label. They're quite inexpensive and pretty darned good.

but here's a small suggestion: If your rifle has iron sights that you're planning to use as a backup system, it isn't essential that you use detachable mounts, but make sure you have whatever screwdrivers or Allen wrenches are required to remove the scope. Likewise if you carry a spare scope!

Selecting the right scope is a complicated and difficult process, and there's really no way I can make it easy for you. There are dozens of brands and myriad power ranges. There are 30mm and one-inch tubes, and numerous diameters of objectives lenses. With apologies, I have to let you sort this out for yourself, but I'll give you a few guidelines. First, in optics, more so than with any other type of sporting equipment that I know of, you get what you pay for. There aren't a lot of real bargains; the market is too competitive for that. On the other hand, you do get good value for your money. As we discussed in a previous chapter, I can't tell you with a straight face that a $7,000 custom rifle is ten times better than a $700 factory rifle. The differences are subtle. I can tell you that there are substantial and discernible differences between a $100 riflescope and a $500 riflescope. The more expensive scope will have better optics and better coatings. You can see better through it, and you can probably see the difference quite readily. You will also find the adjustments to be more precise, and you're almost certainly getting a more rugged and reliable scope.

This is not to say that you must have the most expensive scope on the market. The high-end scopes offer better light-gathering capabilities, more repeatable adjustments, and enhanced clarity, but it depends on your budget. If you can afford the best, fine. If you can't, try to at least stay in the middle range, and avoid the extremely inexpensive scopes. Within any given product line, the more powerful the scope the more costly it will be. You're better off with a somewhat less powerful scope of higher quality than the other way around. Also, if you have to make a choice between a top-of-the-line rifle and a top-of-the-line scope, you will actually get more for your money by going with a higher-quality scope and a medium-priced rifle.

There are many good brands of scopes, and it would be even more confusing if I tried to give you a shopping list. It would also be unfair, because I certainly don't claim to have personal knowledge of all the various makes. Whenever possible, stick with known brand names, and buy the best you can. In addition to the brand, you will need to make decisions regarding the magnification, as well as other characteristics. Let's take a look at some of these.

Right now the trend in scopes is toward higher and higher magnification, mostly in variable scopes with increasingly high upper ranges. Extremely powerful scopes are essential in varmint hunting and helpful in serious long-range shooting, but for general-purpose big-game hunting many shooters are over-scoped. Provided you remember to keep your scope turned down to a low setting unless you really need more, this does no harm. However, more powerful scopes are both heavier and more expensive, and I find it a waste unless you really need it. There's one more thing. Variables up to about 3.5-10X can maintain focus throughout the power range. Variables with high ends much above 10X must have a parallax-adjustment focusing ring on the objective lens. This is just one more thing to worry about when you're getting ready to shoot at game, and most of the time it's unnecessary.

Unless you hunt in very open country most of the time, or you're planning on a lot of serious long-range work, I strongly recommend you stick with variables of no greater power than about 3.5-10X on general-purpose hunting rifles. For most of us, variables of 2-7X, 2.5-8X, the ever-popular 3-9X, or 3.5-10X are suitable for virtually all big-game hunting. It is this class of scope that we will mount on our two .30-06s. If most of your shooting is under 200 yards, you might even question whether you need a variable at all. A

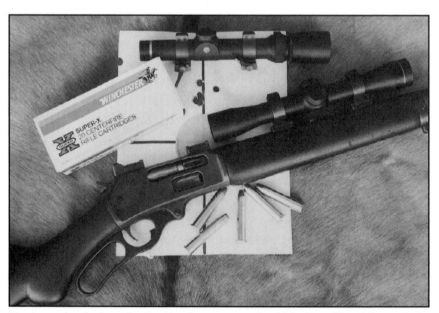

Here's another look at the Jim Brockman-customized Marlin. This rifle carried a whole suite of sight options: Conventional 1.75-5X scope and long-eye-relief 4X, both in Talley detachable mounts; and the peep sight concealed in the rear scope base.

This is a Steiner Hunting-Z 3-9X variable, mounted on a Lazzeroni 8.59 Titan. This scope is relatively compact for a 30mm tube, and it looks good on the big Lazzeroni.

good fixed 4X scope is simple and reliable, and actually offers about all the magnification needed for most big-game hunting.

On a rifle intended for timber shooting, or on a dangerous-game rifle such as a .375, I normally mount something on the order of a 1.75-5X variable. These scopes tend to be wonderfully light and compact, but keep in mind that their typical straight-tubed objective lens (whether one inch or 30mm) cannot gather as much light as a larger objective. The newer 1.5-6X scopes aren't quite as compact, but their larger objective lenses offer a good deal more light-gathering potential.

While we're on the subject, let's talk about objective lenses. Larger objectives do gather more light, but this must be in relationship to the quality of the lenses and coatings. A cheap scope with a big objective bell is just that: a cheap scope with a big objective. However, given high quality throughout, a larger objective does gather more light than a smaller objective, at least

Here's the long and short of scopes: A Leupold 1.75-5X on a .375 H&H; and a new Leupold Premier Scope (LPS) on a .300 Weatherby manufactured by Rifles, Inc. Only you can decide how much scope you need to give you confidence . . . but keep in mind that most of us make short shots far more frequently than long shots.

up to a certain point. The question you must ask is "How much light do you need?" The very large objective lens was developed by Europeans for European hunting, where it makes a great deal of sense. They don't have "shooting hours" as we know them; so long as they can gather enough natural light, including moonlight, for accurate shooting, their custom and convention is to continue the hunt. We don't do that. Our legal shooting hours end within a half-hour after sunset and begin no earlier than a half-hour before sunrise. The light is dim during these critical periods, and we need the light-gathering abilities of a good scope. But there is a limit to how much we need.

The very large objectives do gather light, but they cause two problems. First, they make a scope heavier than it needs to be. Second, and far more insidious, they require the scope to be mounted very high so that the objective clears the barrel. This means that you must either have a very high comb on your stock or, more likely, you must lift your head off the stock to obtain a proper sight picture. I don't think the benefit is worth the cost. I prefer a scope with an objective lens of no more than 44mm. Even more to my taste are objectives from 36 to 42mm.

It's a somewhat related subject, but you must also make a decision between one-inch and 30mm scope tubes. The one-inch tube has long been the American standard, while the larger 30mm tube is more popular in Europe. These days the 30mm tube is becoming increasingly popular over here. All things being equal, the larger tube does gather more light. However, this supposes that 30mm tubes have 30mm *optics*. Many of the 30mm scopes sold in the United States have one-inch optics within, which does absolutely nothing to enhance brightness. There is an advantage to this construction in that the range of adjustment is greatly increased, so some target and varmint scopes are made in this fashion, and are so advertised. Other scopes are made in this fashion but simply advertised as "30mm scopes," so be careful.

Given 30mm tubes and good 30mm optics, the larger tube can gather more light, and can gain benefit from a larger objective. However, the 30mm scopes are heavier and bulkier. I do have good 30mm scopes on several of my rifles, and I like them, but they are not essential, and they will add weight. Take your choice.

One feature you must pay careful attention to is eye relief. Most American scopes are pretty good in this regard, but many European scopes are not. This is because Europeans, accustomed to large objectives, mount their scopes high. They learn to shoot with their heads high. We shoot with our heads down on the stock, which cocks our foreheads closer to the scope. The more powerful the rifle, the more eye relief you need to keep the scope away from your forehead. Take it from one who knows: Eye relief is critical on a hunting rifle scope. At the range, in perfect positions, you can stay away from a scope with minimal eye relief, as little as two inches. But in the field, shooting fast or from unfamiliar positions, you need more. The more felt recoil, the more eye relief you need, which means that you need more eye relief in very light rifles than in rifles of normal weight, regardless of caliber. The worst scope cut I have ever received was from a wooden-stocked .30-06, but I shot it from a cramped prone position atop a rimrock. I got the deer, but I think I bled almost as much as it did! Three inches of eye relief is a good, comfortable amount that will keep the scope away from you under almost all conditions.

Reticles are largely a matter of personal preference, and there are many to choose from these days. In thick cover and on running shots a dot-and-cross hairs offers a very fast, bold aiming point, but at longer ranges the dot obscures too much of the animal for my taste. I think the best all-round reticle available is the "plex"-type, with thicker outer wires and a thinner center. This has become the most popular of all reticles, and with good reason. The plex is fast, bold in poor light, and the thinner inner wires allow precise aiming at all ranges. There are other options, but virtually all of my riflescopes today have a plex reticle. If you want a good, thorough, in-depth coverage of scopes, spotting scopes, and binoculars I recommend my friend John Barsness's new book on optics for the hunter also published by Safari Press.

When it comes to scope mounts, there are many good systems. When properly assembled and installed, virtually all of the standard commercial mounts work very well, especially at normal recoil levels. When you get into heavy recoil—whether from a very light rifle, a large caliber, or, worst of all, the two factors combined—the demands on both scopes and mounts are far greater. Then you need extra-tough mounts, and a higher-quality scope is good insurance. We'll talk about scope mounts in much greater detail in the next chapter. However, let's conclude this discussion with the decision regarding a fixed or a detachable mount, since this directly relates to choice of sights.

Good detachable mounts were extremely rare just a decade ago, but now there are several very repeatable systems. Although detachables seem to be the "in thing" in scope mounts, the only real utility I see in them is on rifles that have open sights, and you actually envision some situation where you might want to use those sights. I do not recommend putting a detachable mount on a rifle just for "looks." This for a couple of reasons. First, detachables are more expensive. Second, although mounts like the Talley, Warne, and Leupold Quick Release are very repeatable, *all* detachables, including European claw mounts, will eventually "wear" and develop a little play if you insist on taking them on and off all the time. If you're going to use the rifle with a scope, leave the scope on the rifle as much as possible. If you have a detachable mount and auxiliary irons, you must sight in the iron sights. Once that's done, put the scope on the rifle, zero it, take it off, then put it back on and shoot it again to make sure it's really repeatable. Then leave it alone.

If your rifle doesn't have iron sights, I see no reason for a detachable mount. There is nothing gained by taking the scope off to transport the rifle. More likely, there is greater risk in damaging the scope by having it loose than by leaving it solidly attached. If you simply must have a detachable mount for esthetics, or if you wish to carry a spare scope pre-zeroed in detachable rings, then put your primary scope on the rifle, zero it, check it, and leave it alone. Today's riflescopes are extremely reliable and rugged, but I believe that the best way to keep them that way is to get them properly mounted and zeroed, and then mess with them as little as possible.

═══ CHAPTER NINE ═══

MOUNTING THE SCOPE

The primary ingredient for accuracy and reliability is the rifle itself—but neither quality can reach its potential without dependable, repeatable sights. In the previous chapter most of the discussion was devoted to riflescopes. This is appropriate, because the telescopic sight is far and away the dominant sight in today's big-game hunting world. I even went so far as to say that quality of scope is more important than quality of rifle. I believe this, but never forget that neither the best rifle nor the best scope is worth a darn unless the two are solidly mated together by a good mount.

Scope mounts are largely taken for granted today. This is probably as it should be; you should be able to mount a scope on a rifle and forget about it. Once mounted, the scope properly becomes part of the rifle, not a separate entity. Just remember that it's the mount that makes this possible!

SCOPE MOUNTS

The scope mount starts with screw holes drilled and tapped into the action. If you start with a military action, such as a Mauser or Springfield, or a "pre-scope-era" commercial action, a gunsmith can readily do this work, but in most cases this has been done for you. Virtually all commercial actions today are drilled and tapped for scope mounts, and most mounts are offered with the proper contours and screw holes to fit. Regardless of which type of mount you choose, make sure you get the right one! The variations of heights and screw arrangements are endless—and some are close enough to almost fit. Almost isn't good enough; obviously the screw holes must line up, but the height at both front and rear must also make the mount parallel to the line of bore, and the mount or mounts must mold to any contour of the action. Check closely; it's all too easy to come home from the gunshop with a mount that's not quite right.

Scope mounts come in a bewildering array of types and styles. The good news is that I don't know of any that don't work . . . up to a point, and only with proper assembly. We'll deal with the latter in a bit. First let's deal with the reliability of scope mounts.

RELIABILITY

Recoil is the scope mount's greatest enemy—also, by the way, the scope's nemesis! The continued pounding of recoil

This is the Conetrol mount, one of the sleekest and lightest scope mounts available. It is also very strong but definitely non-detachable.

tends to loosen screws, and it makes scopes tend to slip forward in the rings. At its worst, recoil can literally shake a mount to pieces. That's the bad news. The good news is that virtually all scope mount systems, if properly assembled, will withstand normal recoil more or less forever. "Normal" recoil is hard to define; recoil depends not only on the sheer size of the cartridge but also on gun weight, bullet weight, velocity, even the weight of the propellant charge. When I think about normal recoil, I'm thinking about something like an eight-pound .30-06, which should generate up to 30 foot-pounds of recoil. This is not a problem for any commercial scope mount. Add power, reduce gun weight—or do both—and recoil goes up. A .300 magnum produces recoil reaching into the forties. This is not a problem. Depending on gun weight, a .338 or .375 gets into the fifties. This is *usually* not a problem, but now we're into the area of caution. A .416 is usually somewhere in the 60-foot-pound class. At this point recoil is serious, and few scope mounts can withstand it for an extended period.

The point is that you should choose your mounting system according to what you need it to do. If you have a standard, versatile hunting cartridge up to about .300 magnum in a rifle of normal weight, you needn't worry. Any decent commercial mount will do fine. If you have a hard kicker, you must narrow your choices. I don't personally believe that "one-piece bases" are inherently stronger than "two-piece bases." Far more important, to my mind, is how the rings mate to the base.

The most common scope mounting system is probably the "Redfield" mount, in quotes because this mounting system is also manufactured by Leupold, B-Square, and others. It consists of a dovetailed extension on the forward ring that twists into a female dovetail on the forward base, while the rear ring is held onto a flat-surfaced base by two opposing windage screws. This mount has tremendous attributes. It is sleek, simple, and good-looking, and the windage screws give it tremendous horizontal adjustment. It is *not* a particularly strong mount. Having said that, I'll add that I have this type of mount on many of my own rifles. I have absolute confidence in it up to .30-06, 7mm magnum recoil levels. I also had a .375 H&H with this type of scope mount. Over the course of more than a decade it gave me absolutely no problems . . . but this mounting system is best left behind before you get to that level of recoil.

Leupold's new Dual Dovetail mount is a variation on the Redfield system in that the Redfield front dovetail is duplicated on the rear mount. You lose the windage-adjustment capability but gain tremendous strength.

Perhaps the second most popular mounting system, and certainly one of the most economical, is the Weaver system. The Weaver scope mount uses rail dovetails and through-bolts to hold the rings on the mounts, and the split rings are held to the scope with a dovetailed clamp on one side and two screws on the other. The good old Weaver mount is, well, just plain ugly. Always was, always will be. It is also very strong and very effective— much stronger than the more attractive Redfield system. If you have a rifle with heavy recoil and you're looking for an inexpensive scope mount that will hold up, don't overlook the Weaver system. Simmons's excellent 4x4 mount is merely a Weaver-type mount modified so as to be detachable and repeatable. Leupold's new QRW (Quick Release, Weaver style) is another variation.

Beyond these two most common systems are many other options. The "stud" mount, Australian-designed but later manufactured by Tasco, is a very sturdy system. Leupold's QR (Quick Release) mount borrows from the "ring stud-into-mount" concept to create a very simple and very repeatable detachable mount. Perhaps the sleekest and lightest mounting system on the market today is the Conetrol. The Conetrol rings are split vertically rather than horizontally, with the two halves joined on top by a dovetailed cap and held together at the bottom by the base itself. Conetrol, while light, is an exceptionally strong system, and I rate it one of the best. If it has drawbacks, they are the fact that it's a difficult mount for fumble-fingered folks like me to assemble,

The Talley detachable mount with two-screw rings is one of the best "over-the-counter" detachable mounts. It is extremely repeatable, and will hold up well beyond .375 H&H recoil levels.

and that, once assembled, the scope is simply not coming off the rifle under field conditions!

Both Ruger and Sako offer integral mounting systems. They are similar in that split rings, under screw pressure, clamp to integral dovetails manufactured as part of the rifle. Neither is detachable *per se*, but both can be readily modified to be detachable by a decent gunsmith or skilled hobbyist. These are both very good systems, and the scope mount industry can be thankful more manufacturers haven't followed suit!

There are undoubtedly some other mounting systems I have missed, but these are the most common non-detachable systems. These days interest in detachable mounts is at an all-time high, and there are quite a few good ones. As stated in the previous chapter, I have reservations about detachable mounts. It isn't that I don't like them. I like them very much, but I don't trust them nearly as much as fixed mounts. I think they are best

This is the custom detachable mount on my .416 Rigby. The bar between the rings can be tightened as the mount wears, ensuring repeatability throughout the life of the rifle.

treated as "backup detachable," rather than subjecting them to constant attachment and reattachment—and I think most of us are best served by making well-considered decisions about when and whether they should be used. That said, we have better, cheaper, and more available detachable mounts than ever right now—but just like fixed mounts, the more recoil there is, the more careful you must be.

This matter is compounded by the fact that detachable mounts are most often desired on heavy-recoiling rifles. Most systems will work very well on rifles up to .375 H&H or so . . . but there are very few mounts of any type that will keep a scope on recoil machines like the .460 Weatherby Magnum, .505 Gibbs, and similar big boomers. As an example, I had a .416 Hoffman (the wildcat forerunner of the .416 Remington Magnum). That's not such a big deal; such a cartridge would normally have recoil foot-pounds in the sixties, and a lot of mounts will handle such recoil. Unfortunately (for my shoulder!) this rifle was built as a "swamp gun," with a light synthetic stock and a barrel that was mostly hole. It weighed about 6½ pounds and almost certainly delivered 100 foot-pounds of recoil. I had a terrible time keeping a scope on this rifle. It ate up mount after mount, including several very good ones.

You will not run into this difficulty on "normal" rifles with "normal" recoil. The Warne detachable mounts work extremely well up to at least .375 H&H. The Talley mount system does wonderfully up to the .416s (with normal gun weight) and beyond. I don't yet have an opinion as to the normal limits of the Leupold QR and QRW or the Simmons 4x4, but I'm sure they will hold up to at least .375 H&H.

At some level—and I'm not exactly sure where that is—no "standard" mounts will be totally foolproof. Gunsmiths often modify existing mounts by drilling and tapping for larger-diameter hardened screws, which helps. And there are custom mounts. These can be very expensive, but at high recoil levels the answers are rarely simple. My John Rigby .416, for instance, has a detachable side mount with the front base milled into the action bridge and the rear base milled into the action wall. As an optional feature, the mount may cost hundreds of dollars, but it is totally repeatable, and I don't have to worry about it.

My David Miller 7mm Remington Magnum, on the other hand, has exactly the opposite of a detachable mount. Miller's special mount is actually a scope harness milled from a solid (and huge) block of solid steel and fitted precisely to both rifle and scope. The mount cannot shift. As proof of that, I've had my Miller rifle for more than a decade, and it has never shifted zero a quarter-inch. On the other hand, there is no easy removal of the scope, and if the existing 3.5-10X Leupold ever gives up the ghost, the tolerances are so tight that there is no guarantee a replacement scope of current manufacture will fit!

Before going hunting I *always* check a rifle's zero. I recommend you do the same. I also always try to check the rifle's zero when I get to camp. Sometimes circumstances don't allow— but this I will tell you: Failing to check zero after traveling, at whatever altitude and humidity at which you will be hunting, is an invitation to disaster! Usually the rifle is fine, or at least very close to fine. But sometimes it is not.

After decades in this game, I have just three scoped rifles that I can absolutely rely upon to be "in zero" at any time. One is my David Miller 7mm Remington Magnum, with Miller's milled scope harness fitted to rifle and scope. Another is my John Rigby .416, with its custom detachable mount. The third is my beat-up old .375, a left-hand-converted pre-'64 Model 70 that has seen much better days. Its final mount—I think the fourth mount it has worn in the eighteen years I've owned it—is a Talley detachable mount in two-screw rings. Significant is that I sent the rifle to Dave Talley, and he *fitted* the mount to the rifle, meaning that all the screw holes line up precisely. Talley mounts and rings are available "over the counter," and they work very well, but actions vary by microscopic and yet measurable amounts, and in detachable mounts—and all mounts at high recoil levels—exact fit becomes the difference between failure and reliability.

This book is not about scope mounts for ultralight .416s or behemoth .505 Gibbs rifles. This book is about setting up "normal" rifles for hunting. I interpret this to mean rifles ranging from the 6mms up through the .30s (magnum and standard), and perhaps up to the .33s, .35s, and maybe the .375. That simplifies things tremendously. *With proper assembly* most scope mounting systems will hold together indefinitely within this caliber range.

I cannot give you step-by-step instructions for each and every type of mount. For one thing, there simply isn't space. For another, I don't claim to have even seen, let alone assembled, all the various types of scope mounts. I will talk you through how I scoped the two "test" Model 700s I have acquired for this book. But first let me give you the three most common reasons for mount failure— and the ways to avoid them.

COMMON REASONS FOR MOUNT FAILURE

Improper Assembly

This is the single most significant scope mount bugaboo. The answer is simple: *Read the directions.* I know it is "un-macho" to do so, but there is no other way. Read them and *follow them.* Here's a good example. The directions for the common Redfield mounting system tell you that you should install the bases, then "turn in" the front ring by attaching it to a one-inch (or 30mm) dowel. *Then* you attach the bottom half of the rear ring and set in the scope, making sure it's aligned with the rings and action. We all know that the easy and fast way to do this is: Install the bases.

Before mounting a scope, make sure you have everything you need: screwdrivers, Loc-Tite, a bit of sandpaper for roughing the rings. Make certain the mount fits properly— and then read the directions before you start.

Attach the front ring to the scope, and loosely attach the rear ring to the scope. Remove one windage screw. Use the scope to "turn in" the front ring, and guide the rear base into the remaining windage screw. I've mounted dozens of scopes by this method, as have many of you. Wrong!

Chances are the front ring isn't quite square, so when you're all finished you have lopsided pressure on the scope. Worse, this mounting system relies on the bottom of the rear ring being absolutely square against the top of the rear base. This is very difficult to achieve by the "quick" method. I have seen many rifles mounted with the Redfield system that show daylight between the base and the bottom of the rear ring. Sooner or later they will let go. Many scope mounting systems allow shortcuts. Avoid them and *follow the directions.*

Loosening of Screws

This is a touchy subject. It isn't a matter of making sure the screws are tight enough; it's relatively easy to break off screws by overtightening, and then you've got a real mess on your hands. Rather, what's important is to get the screws—both mount and ring—nice and snug without breaking them. Believe me, I'm speaking from the standpoint of a guy who has broken *lots* of screws!

The answer is to use a screw-securing compound like Loc-Tite. I generally use Uncle Mike's "Gun-Tite," which bonds the screws in place but can still be broken free with relative ease if you want to remove the scope and/or mounts. I will freely admit that I don't always Loc-Tite the screws into place at light recoil levels—but if I'm planning on hunting with the rifle, or it has relatively high recoil, I *always* do!

Scope Shifting Forward

This is one of the most misunderstood facets of rifle physics. Newton's Law says that for every action there is an equal and opposite reaction. When the bullet goes forward, the rifle goes

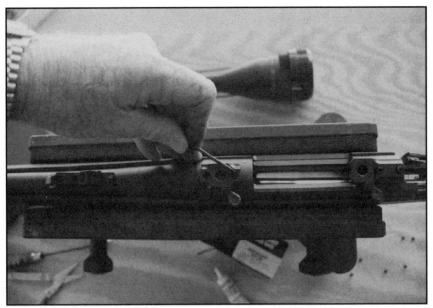

Regardless of the type of mount, the first step is to install the bases. Make certain you use the right screws for front and rear, and if you have any doubts, try them before you Loc-Tite them into place.

rearward. That's recoil. However, the scope is not the rifle, although it's attached to same. When the rifle goes rearward it tries to leave the scope behind, with the effect that the scope tends to move forward. As with most problems, this is not significant at "normal" recoil levels. But when recoil becomes severe—or the scope is heavy—forward movement is a common problem. This is much more pronounced with the heavy 30mm scopes and the large high-range variables that are becoming popular today.

Detachable mounts such as the Warne and Talley often have a "recoil shoulder" for the bottom of the ring to butt against. Misguided logic says this shoulder should be to the rear. This is wrong. Scope movement under recoil is *forward* so the shoulder should be to the front and the ring should butt up tightly to it. In the fall of '97 I went on a "writers' elk hunt" with the new Beretta Mato rifle. All the "issue" rifles were the synthetic version—

This is the Leupold ring wrench, a very simple tool that makes installing rings into Redfield-type bases very simple. Lacking the wrench, you must assemble the ring and use a one-inch (or 30mm) dowel to turn in the ring. Do not use your scope.

relatively light. All the calibers were fairly stout—.300 and .338 Winchester Magnums. All the scopes were Swarovski PH 30mm models, bright and clear but reasonably heavy. All of the scopes were installed with Talley detachable mounts—but each and every mount was installed backward, with the recoil shield to the rear. Yep, every scope was shifting forward under recoil. The long-term fix was to reverse the mounts, but this wouldn't necessarily stop the scopes from shifting forward in the rings. The immediate fix, which instantly worked, was to Loc-Tite all the ring screws. This is always a good idea, but it's darn near essential when you get above the .270/.30-06 level of recoil—or if you're using a heavy scope. Equally important as Loc-Tite on the screws is to take emery paper and rough up the inner surfaces of the scope rings before assembly. This will greatly assist the rings in getting a grip on the scope and, with the ring screws properly tightened, should prevent slippage. Once you have roughed up the surfaces, you can put a bit of Loc-Tite on the inner surfaces of the rings as well. As a bit of insurance, Geoff Miller also puts a drop of clear nail varnish on the forward edge of a scope roughly touching the scope. If this 'seal" is broken, your scope is shifting on the rings!

STEP-BY-STEP SCOPE MOUNTING

Again, the exact procedure varies quite a bit from one type of scope mount to another, but the basics remain pretty much the same. Scope mounting is not rocket science. Working alone in my garage, it took me less than an hour to mount scopes on *both* of our Model 700s. Much of this time was spent in taking pictures along the way. I'm not a very handy guy, and I don't warrant the work to be perfect, but I expect both sets of mounts to work for a long time.

As you probably expected, I decided on two "general purpose" scopes to add versatility to these two .30-06 rifles. I settled on a Leupold 2.5-8X and a Redfield 3-9X. Neither is a new scope; I've had both on other rifles, and I know they work. Completely arbitrarily, I decided to put the Leupold on the synthetic-stocked rifle and the Redfield on the older walnut-stocked gun. Choice of mounts was not quite so arbitrary.

Both rifles wear iron sights, but (as mentioned previously) the comb on the walnut-stocked rifle is so high that I can "see" the iron sights only with great difficulty. So I decided to mount this rifle with non-detachable Redfield-type mounts. The actual brand used was Leupold, but this system varies but little from one manufacturer to another. I can see the iron sights much more readily on the synthetic-stocked rifle, so I decided to use one of the new detachable mounts, in this case the Leupold QR.

Virtually all mount manufacturers offer a variety of ring heights. Choice depends largely on the diameter of your scope's objective lens; the mount must be high enough so the objective lens clears the action, barrel, and rear sight (if present). I like to mount a scope as low as possible, but this also depends on height of comb. The height you want is the one that will allow a full field of view with the gun properly shouldered and cheeked. Again, every scope mount system is different, but here's a quick sketch of how I mounted the scopes using these two systems.

The Universal Steps

These are things that you should do with any and all scope mounting systems.

(1) Gather your tools.

First make sure you have everything you need. Rifle, scope, bases, and rings are obvious. You also need proper screwdrivers. Most mounts today use Allen wrenches, and most manufacturers supply an Allen wrench. You will also need a very small-blade screwdriver to remove the guard screws, and with many mounting systems (like the Redfield type) you will need a fairly large-blade screwdriver. Make sure you also have a bit of emery paper, some Loc-Tite, and alcohol (or a similar substance) for degreasing. For the Redfield-type mount you will need something on the order of a one-inch dowel to twist the front mount onto the base. You can often use a screwdriver handle, but *don't* plan on using your scope!

(2) Read the directions.

This is probably the most important step of all . . . and usually the one that we overlook until we get in trouble. Read the directions carefully, make sure you understand them, and *follow them.*

(3) Degrease all components.

Most scope mounts come from the factory with a heavy coating of oil to prevent rust while they sit on dealers' shelves. This oil must be removed or your mount is likely to loosen no matter what else you do. Isopropyl or wood alcohol works just fine, as do commercial degreasing solvents. Midway Arms offers a good one in an aerosol can.

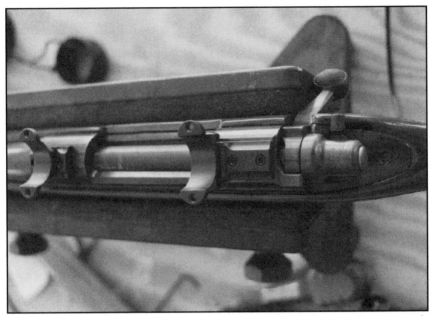

On a Redfield-type mount, one of the real tricks is to center the rear ring as precisely as possible—and make absolutely certain the windage-adjustment screws get a good bite into the dovetails on the ring.

(4) Rough up the inner surfaces of the rings.

These days some mount rings have ribbed inner surfaces, which help, but many rings have inner surfaces that are highly polished and smooth. You may not be able to tighten the ring enough to prevent forward slippage of the scope during recoil. This problem can usually be cured by taking fine emery paper and roughing up the inner surface of the rings. Don't go overboard; you certainly don't want to remove any metal, just create a surface that will offer more friction between ring and scope.

(5) Use a solid platform.

Always put the rifle in a padded vise or gun-cleaning rest.

(6) Loc-Tite your screws.

As you go, use just a wee bit of Loc-Tite or similar bonding material to help hold the screws in place. This is most important on the mount screws, but I prefer to Loc-Tite the ring screws as well. Make sure you use a brand that can be broken free readily! "Gun Tite" from Michaels of Oregon is the most common brand. Just put a small drop on the tip of the screw, in the thread, and make sure it flows all the way around the screw. This is a wee bit of insurance that can make a very big difference.

Specific Steps for Redfield-type Mount

First, follow the universal steps 1-6 above. Then:

(7) Install the bases.

There are no tricks here; simply lay the base or bases on the action and screw it (them) down. One caution: The screw lengths may be different between the front and rear base, and the instructions may not say which is which since this is likely to vary from one action to another. If you have any question, put the screws in first without Loc-Tite to make sure you have it right. While you're at it, make absolutely certain the action will still function when the screws are fully tightened. Once in a while you run into a situation where an overly long mount screw will protrude through the action and bind against the bolt. This is usually, but not always, caused by using the wrong screw, like a rear-base screw on a front base. Obviously a screw that does this must be shortened or replaced with a shorter screw. When you're sure of the proper screw arrangement, put them in with Loc-Tite and get them good and snug.

(8) Install the front ring.

Leupold makes a nifty and inexpensive nylon "ring wrench" that makes this simple. Failing that, install the two halves of

When you tighten the rings, tighten each side a bit at a time. Chances are neither side will quite bottom out, and that's OK—what you care about is a good grip on the scope.

the forward ring around a one-inch (or 30mm, depending on ring size) dowel. You can cheat by using a screwdriver or other tool handle. Insert the male dovetail on the ring into the female dovetail on the base, and twist it into place. The idea is to get it as perfectly square as you possibly can. When this step is finished, only the bottom half of the front ring should be in place.

(9) Install the rear ring.
Remove one of the windage screws and set the bottom half of the rear ring tight against the remaining screw, ensuring that the half-moon dovetail in the ring is mated to the inner surface of the screwhead. Install the other windage screw. The idea is to get the rear ring centered as precisely as possible in the middle of the base. You will probably need to

loosen one screw and tighten the other a couple of times to accomplish this.

(10) Install the scope.
Lay the scope in the bottom halves of the rings. With it in place, make sure that both rings are at right angles to the long axis of the scope.

(11) Attach the top halves of the rings.
Alternately tightening one screw and then the other, *loosely* secure the scope.

(12) Check eye relief and cross hairs.
At this point, take the rifle out of the vise or rest and make certain the cross hairs are exactly horizontal and vertical and that the eye relief is where you want it. The former is not as easy as it sounds; I often wind up with a scope that's very slightly canted. You can do it "by eye" by aligning the vertical reticle with a telephone pole or the corner of a building, or there are several inexpensive little gadgets available for ensuring a scope is properly leveled. However you do it, get it right—and put the scope as far forward as you can and still obtain a full field of view.

(13) Tighten the rings.
With the scope properly positioned, get the rings good and snug. Don't expect the two halves of the rings to join perfectly. They probably will not. Instead, try to keep any gaps between the two halves about the same on both sides by tightening each screw a bit at a time, rather than completely tightening one side and then the other. Note that it is relatively easy to break off ring screws by overtightening. Get them good and snug, but don't overdo it!

That's all there is to it on the Redfield system. This is a very easy mount to install, and I suppose I've done it many dozens of times.

Next, I turned to the Leupold QR system. This was actually the first time I had ever installed a QR mount. I have to say that this is the quickest, simplest, and easiest mount installation I have ever done.

Specific Steps for Leupold Quick Release System

First, follow the universal steps 1-6 . Then step 7 from the Redfield mount steps. (The only potential catch is to make certain you have the release levers facing to the rear.) Then continue with:

(8) Install the bottom halves of the rings.

The beauty of this system is that all the work is done for you. All you have to do is drop the bottom half of the ring into the base, making sure that the dovetailed slot faces to the rear. Then tighten the lever.

Then continue to follow the Redfield mount steps 9 through 13 listed above. That's all there is to it!

Again, every commercial system differs slightly. The real key is to follow the directions, and if you do, you can't get into too much trouble. Once in a great while, with any commercial rifle and any commercial mount, you will run into a bizarre problem, usually associated with off-center screw holes. A different type of mount may work, but in extreme cases a gunsmith may need to modify the mount or drill new holes for the bases. Remember that one of the great advantages to the old Redfield system, even though it is not the strongest mount, is that windage adjustments can be made in the base. When sighting in a rifle with a scope mounted by this system, it's best to make the initial windage adjustments with the base rather than the scope's internal adjustments. Problems are rare. I didn't expect any with these Model 700s, and I didn't encounter any. Now the rifles are scoped, and it's almost time to start shooting.

CHAPTER TEN

BEDDING IS ABOUT VIBRATION

Proper bedding of a stock is often considered some sort of mysterious "black art." It's really a very simple concept, but its execution is greatly complicated by the fact that there are several solutions . . . and no two rifles are alike in the way they respond to these various options.

Bedding is not about the fit of the action and barrel into the stock. That's inletting. Bedding is about dampening or controlling the barrel's vibration to optimize accuracy. All barrels vibrate while the bullet travels down the bore, sort of like the oscillation of a high-pressure water hose. The purpose of barrel bedding is to ensure that the microscopic—but very real—vibrating movement of the barrel is the same from shot to shot, so that the barrel is in the same position each time a bullet exits. During firing the forces of recoil also exert tremendous stress on the action. The purpose of action bedding, therefore, is to ensure that the action is mated squarely with the barrel, and that no shifting occurs from shot to shot.

Altering the barrel bedding is often one of the first things considered when a rifle isn't shooting the way the shooter thinks it should. It should probably be one of the last things considered. We will discuss this in much greater detail in chapter 13, "Troubleshooting Accuracy." For now, let's just say that barrel bedding is only one of several factors that may prevent a rifle

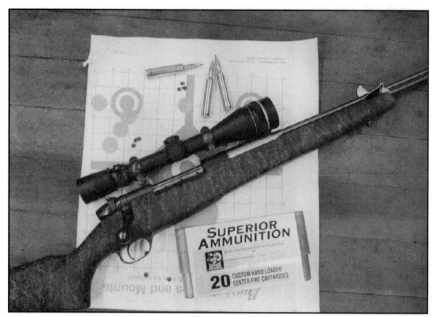

This .30-.378 Weatherby was classic in the way it responded to upward pressure. Note the cardboard sticking out between barrel and fore-end; that's all that was required to change it from the awful group below the rifle to the super group above!

from optimizing its accuracy. Many rifles *will* shoot better with a revamped or radically different bedding system . . . but if there's a problem, that may not be it!

Once in a while you'll find an off-the-shelf rifle with a serious barrel-bedding problem, such as a warped stock that bears on one side of the barrel channel. If this is the case, accuracy is likely to be abysmal, and relieving the pressure may instantly shrink group size dramatically. Failing a serious problem, changing the bedding *can* (not *will*) yield accuracy improvement that ranges from slight to substantial, but only rarely will it be dramatic. As we discussed in chapter 7, quality of barrel remains the primary contributor to accuracy, and as we will see in subsequent chapters, matching good ammo to that barrel is also of primary importance. Again, barrel bedding is not a cure-all and is just one of many factors contributing to accuracy.

The tendency is to attack the barrel channel with chisel and fiberglass, but action bedding is also extremely important. If the action has sloppy bedding and can shift even very slightly during recoil, it doesn't much matter how well the barrel channel is bedded; you can't maximize accuracy. Worse, an action that is shifting under recoil will almost certainly split a wooden stock sooner or later, depending on how much shifting and how much recoil.

Most factory rifles use machine inletting that today can be cut to close enough tolerances so that screw pressure (through-bolts on most two-piece stocks; action screws on most bolt-actions) will hold the action in place. Most rifles that are at or above .300 magnum levels of recoil are reinforced with a recoil lug. This lug is generally at the forward edge of the action, but barrel- mounted recoil lugs are used by some manufacturers. Most wooden stocks intended for rifles with substantial recoil are reinforced by crossbolts. The usual placement is behind the

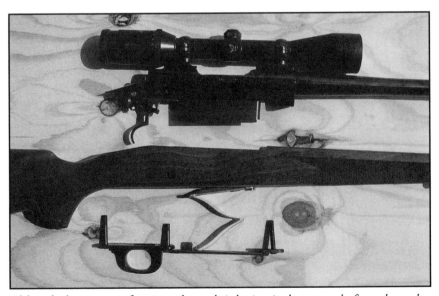

Although the two are often interchanged, inletting is the removal of wood or other stock material so that the action and barrel will nestle into the wood. Bedding is a much more precise science that attempts to control barrel vibration.

magazine box, behind the recoil lug, or both. I just took apart a new Winchester Model 70 Classic in .338 Winchester Magnum, and it serves as a good example.

This rifle has a recoil lug on the bottom forward edge of the action. There is just one crossbolt, through the web of wood remaining between the rear of the magazine box and the front of the trigger assembly. At this level of recoil, that should be fine. To my eye it appears as though the bulk of the inletting has been done by machine, with very little handwork; it looks pretty clean, but there are still some telltale chips and router marks along the action walls and the cut for the trigger assembly. This inletting has apparently been sealed with a urethane or similar coating. So far so good.

Of greatest significance, the cut for the recoil lug and the area where the rear action screw joins the tang have been glass-bedded. This is good. A recoil lug is fine, but is totally useless if it doesn't make firm contact with the stock over as broad an area as possible. Likewise the tang area. This is one of two

This Winchester Model 70 has a single recoil lug at the forward end of the action, a fairly typical arrangement. If it isn't tightly bedded into the stock accuracy will surely suffer.

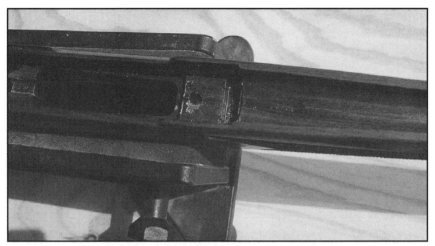

Although this Model 70 is a mass-produced rifle, somebody has gone to work with bedding compound. The inletting for the recoil lug has been nicely bedded and reinforced with fiberglass.

areas where any shifting is most likely to start cracking the wood. The other extremely fragile area in wooden stocks is that little web of wood left between the magazine box and the trigger assembly. In the Model 70, a third action screw bears against this web. This area has not been glassed, but the web is reinforced by the crossbolt. The work on this particular rifle is very sound, and so long as the action screws are kept tight, there should be no shifting and no splitting.

Note that synthetic stocks neither warp nor split, and are usually not reinforced with crossbolts because the stock is stronger without them. However, the requirement for the action to be held in place without shifting remains if you want consistent accuracy.

The way to check for action bedding is to simply do what I just did: Take the action out of the stock and see what you've got. You can usually tell whether the screws, the rear of the magazine box, the tang area, and the recoil lug (if present) are bearing properly. If it appears that there may be shifting in any of these areas, then you can do just what the Winchester factory did on this Model 70. You can remove some stock material and

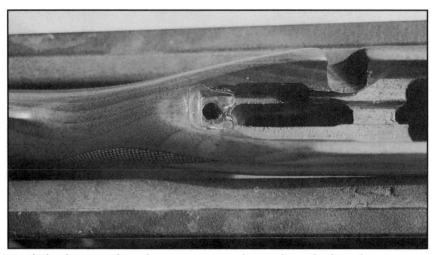

Similarly, the area where the tang mates to the wood—and where the tang screw holds everything together—has received a bit of glassing. Although this was minor handwork, it did the job; this rifle, a .338, is quite accurate.

fill in with a fiberglass bedding compound to create a tight fit. However, there's a caution here. Do-it-yourself bedding is not quite as easy as it sounds. Gunsmiths simply love the over-the-counter bedding kits. It's easy to mess up, and the result tends to create a lot of business for them! I happen to know that I'm not handy enough to attempt it, so if I'm certain I've identified a bedding problem, I take it down the street to a gunsmith. It's a lot easier to get it right the first time!

Again, action bedding is primarily a matter of bearing surface and even pressure to prevent shifting and spread out recoil. Barrel bedding is quite a bit different. The purpose here is to control that firehose of a barrel. There are several different approaches. Every gunmaker—major manufacturer, custom 'smith, or hobbyist—has his or her favorite technique. All of them work, but where the waters get muddied is that every rifle is different and every barrel is an individual. No barrel responds exactly the same to variations in bedding.

Let's start with two opposite approaches—fully bedded and free-floated. "Fully bedded" means that the entire barrel channel is precisely fitted to the barrel. Actually fitting the stock material to the barrel can only be done by hand, a slow and painstaking process. No major manufacturers attempt this, but many custom makers do. A variation of this technique is "glass bedded." Instead of using the glass in a few high-stress areas, as is the case with my Model 70 .338, stock material is removed and bedding compound dumped in. Then the barreled action is dropped in, and the bedding compound hardens in an exact impression of the metal.

Glass bedding obviously requires much less handwork than physically mating wood to metal. Actions are often "fully glassed" by semi-custom and custom makers, and many barrels are bedded in this fashion.

Whether fully bedded in wood or glass, the effect is to dampen the vibration. The opposite approach is free-floating. This is properly termed "lack of bedding" rather than a bedding technique. The barrel rides free in its channel and is not touched anywhere by the stock. With this treatment, the barrel vibrates naturally and will do what it will. Many barrels do shoot very well when free-floated. From a manufacturing standpoint, this is the simplest

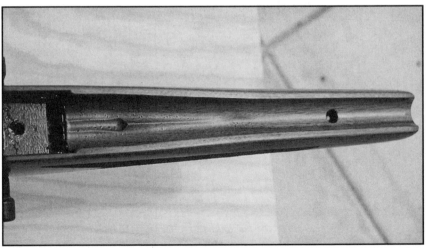

The barrel channel on this same Model 70 is far from perfect, but so long as there isn't uneven pressure it doesn't have to be. What matters is that the rifle shoots consistently, and this one does.

and cheapest "bedding technique"—just hog out the barrel channel enough so that contact is avoided, and you're done. If the gap is extreme (and in some factory rifles it has been) the result is ugly, and can even allow debris to creep in and create pressure. But free-floating can work.

My impression is that the stiffer (heavier) the barrel, the more likely it is to shoot well when free-floated. The thinner the barrel, the more radical its vibration, and the less likely it is to shoot its best without contact. A compromise position on normal sporter-weight barrels (rarely on pencil-thin lightweights) is to bed the first few inches of the barrel (and preferably the action as well), then free-float the rest of the barrel.

Virtually all barrel bedding lies somewhere between fully bedded and free-floated. Bedding can be done with wood or with fiberglass, or it can be done with aluminum or some other solid

Free-floating is far and away the least expensive bedding technique, so it has been adopted by many major manufacturers. It works well for many barrels, but not all. The trick is to avoid contact, but create the minimal gap possible. The fit is bit loose on this particular rifle.

Many very accurate rifles are bedded for the first few inches of the barrel, then free-floated the rest of the way. This Rifles, Inc. .300 Weatherby has a stiff fluted barrel. The action and first three inches of the barrel are glass-bedded, while the rest is free-floated. It shoots very well, so the technique works on this rifle.

material; "pillar bedding" or aluminum block bedding is really just a variation. Another popular variation (and my favorite bedding technique) is "pressure bedding." Pressure bedding involves a buildup of wood, fiberglass, aluminum, or whatever at the fore-end tip so that, when the action screws are good and tight, the fore-end exerts a few pounds of upward pressure on the barrel.

I am not enough of a physicist to properly explain why this works, but it often (never say "always" in matters related to barrels) seems to dampen or control a barrel's vibrations so that group sizes shrink measurably. The great old pre-1964 Model 70 was traditionally bedded in this manner. This was one of the laments when the post-1964 Model 70 was introduced, which touted free-floated barrels and exhibited a really gross barrel-to-channel gap. Many custom gunmakers prefer this pressure-bedding. It is easier than fully bedding; the presence of a pad or pillar near the fore-end tip obviously prevents much of the rest of the barrel from making contact in the channel.

Pressure-bedding is no more a sure-cure than anything else, but many barrels respond well to it, and it's by far the easiest bedding variation to test. You need to do this on the range, using whatever ammo seems to produce the best groups. Just undo the action screws enough to slip a business card between fore-end tip and barrel, then retighten the screws and shoot another group.

This is almost as easy as it sounds. However, like everything else barrel-related, this is not an exact science. If the barrel has been grossly free-floated it may take *several* business cards to create enough pressure. There is also no rule as to how much pressure is enough or how much is too much. Typical is about 5 to 7 pounds, but every rifle is different. You need to experiment with increasing thicknesses of shims, and you should also move them back and forth slightly within the last 3 or 4 inches of the barrel channel.

Sometimes the improvement is dramatic. Just recently Geoff Miller and I were on the range with a new .30-378 Weatherby Magnum. It was shooting OK with its barrel free-floated in a synthetic stock, but we experimented with a shim just to see what would happen. This was one of those rare first-round hits. One cardboard shim just behind the fore-end tip and, *voilà*, the group size was cut in half. Don't expect that kind of improvement all the time. In fact, don't anticipate *any* improvement—but it's always worth a try!

If the shim works, there are several ways to make it permanent. You can build up a fiberglass pad that duplicates the pressure, which is difficult. You can soak the right thickness of business cards or matchbook covers in oil so they won't draw moisture and cut them to fit, which is easy. Or you can use flexible plastic or thin sheets of brass or aluminum, which are more permanent.

There are no hard-and-fast rules regarding bedding and accuracy, but anything that creates uneven pressure anywhere along the barrel channel is likely to be a problem. For instance, although it's one of the slickest and best-looking rifles ever made, the Ruger

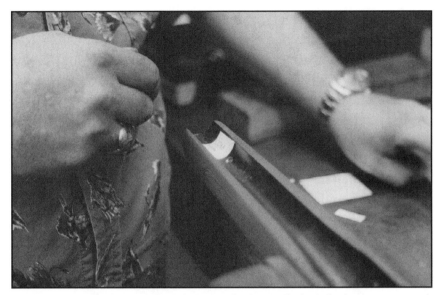

Geoff Miller fits a business card shim into the fore-end of a rifle that was previously free-floated. The card isn't permanent, but you can experiment with various thicknesses and exact placement before setting it into place more permanently.

Number One is rarely a tackdriver, especially in the lighter-barreled models. The two-piece stock is often blamed, but the real culprit is more likely to be the fore-end screw, which mates it to the barrel at about the midpoint of the fore-end. Custom gunmakers who work with the Number One usually change this barrel hanger arrangement in order to improve accuracy.

Similarly, the good old Winchester Model 88 rotary-bolt lever-action uses a mid-fore-end barrel screw. When Geoff Miller started making his Rogue River custom rifles on the 88 action, the first thing he did was design a new barrel hanger that dovetailed into the thickest portion of the barrel just ahead of the action. Mind you, he uses match-grade barrels, and the importance of a good barrel must not be underestimated, but with better barrels, a different hanger, and pressure-bedding his lever-actions routinely deliver sub-half-inch groups.

The full-length Mannlicher-style stocks, though very attractive, are a bedding nightmare, and most of them tend to be so-so in accuracy. The typical arrangement is a bedded channel, with the barrel "clamped" at the muzzle by a steel Schnabel. I had a very beautiful Mannlicher-stocked .270 with a fairly stiff 20-inch barrel bedded in this fashion. It strung its shots vertically, with the bullets climbing two or three inches per shot. In other words, beautiful though it was, it was hopeless to hunt with. The action was well bedded and the barrel channel was lightly glassed and beautifully done. It had a good barrel, and it should have done much better.

I wish I could remember where I got the idea so I could give proper credit; this surely wasn't my idea. Anyway, somebody suggested that I shim the barrel at about the midpoint. Now, although the shim is in about the same place as pressure-bedding, in a Mannlicher with a fore-end-tip Schnabel the effect is altogether different. With the barrel clamped at the muzzle and a shim at the midpoint, the shim is in effect bowing the barrel upward at the shim. Sounds crazy, but that .270 instantly became a minute-of-angle rifle. I replaced the cardboard with a small rectangle of vinyl, cut to fit, and I never touched it again. That rifle was eventually stolen nearly twenty years later. In the time I owned it I never touched the shim, and the accuracy never deteriorated!

Since then I've used that same treatment on other erratic Mannlichers, and it usually works. Unfortunately this is no more a sure-cure than any other fix. So many factors contribute to accuracy that it is extremely unwise to assume that rebedding will answer the mail. Many barrels will deliver about the same results whether free-floated, fully glassed, or pressure-bedded—and you can spend a great deal of time and/or a fair amount of money determining this! Working with the bedding is one possibility in improving performance, but just one. Keep this in mind before you jump in with routers, chisels, sandpaper, and fiberglass.

═══ CHAPTER ELEVEN ═══

FUNCTIONING FOUL-UPS

Reliability is the single most important factor in a hunting rifle. Accuracy is nice, but even if a rifle produces terrible groups of four to six inches it will suffice for the vast majority of shots at big game. Gun fit is extremely important, as are good sights, and calibers and bullets appropriate to the game. But none of these matter at all unless the rifle will feed, fire, extract, and eject with 100 percent reliability. And, while we're at it, the safety must be totally reliable as well.

Functioning foul-ups are relatively rare on new factory rifles, but once in a while a "lemon" can slip through. Problems are much more common with used rifles. (Remember, there's always a reason a used rifle is for sale!) They're even more common when a factory rifle has been altered in any way.

This chapter is not intended as a do-it-yourself guide for fixing problems. I am not a gunsmith, and I don't expect you to be one. Some of us are handy enough to take care of some simple problems, but most of us are not. Instead, the following is intended to assist in isolating and identifying problems. The normal cure, and the one that I strongly suggest, is to take mechanical problems to a competent gunsmith *or* the manufacturer's warranty repair facility. Some problems are interrelated, but let's attack them in terms of these major functional areas: feeding, firing, extraction, ejection, and mechanical safety.

FEEDING

A repeating rifle, regardless of action type, should feed the cartridges into the chamber smoothly. However, this presupposes two things. First, the ammunition must be correct. Second, the magazine must be loaded correctly. One can normally assume that a rifle will handle standard factory loads of the proper caliber. Once in a while, however, problems crop up—especially with more obscure cartridges. For instance, I had a European .416 Rigby that was made before Federal started loading that cartridge. I was delighted when Federal introduced the round—but not overly pleased when I discovered that my rifle wouldn't chamber Federal .416 Rigby ammo. The chamber, apparently reamed for European ammo made to different specs, was a few thousandths too short, and had to be opened up.

It is much more common to run into ammunition problems with handloads. Some chambers run "tight," so that even full-length-resized cases are sticky. Semiautos are particularly prone to this, and the reloading companies offer "small base" dies to fix the problem. Even more common is a length problem. When handloading, we often want to seat the bullet well out of the case so that it almost kisses the lands. This usually aids accuracy, but with some bullets in some rifles, the result will be cartridges too long to fit into the magazine. You need to make sure that the overall length of your cartridges will fit your magazine.

Since different bullets have different shapes, even in the same weight and caliber, you also must ensure that your bullets aren't seated too long for the chamber. I once loaded two different brands of 250-grain bullets for a .340 Weatherby—a "normal" bullet for practice and a "super premium" for a bear hunt. The ogives (the portion of the bullet that curves toward the tip) were different enough that, though both bullets fit perfectly in the magazine, the super-premium bullet stuck in the lands when I chambered a round. Upon extraction the bullet stayed and the case came out, dumping powder into the action and making a real mess.

While there should be no compromise in reliability, it is absolutely true that the farther you are from home (or the nearest replacement) the more critical reliability becomes. On a backpack sheep hunt a gun problem can mean the end of the hunt.

The cure for these unnecessary ills is simple. In a safe place—for instance, on the range, with the rifle pointed downrange—cycle every cartridge you plan to hunt with from the magazine into the chamber and back out. This procedure checks feeding, extraction, and ejection, and failure to do this as part of any pre-hunt or pre-season preparation is a serious mistake.

This is also a good way to ensure that you know how to properly load your magazine. Tubular magazines are pretty goof-proof (one at a time, brass goes in last!). Some box magazines, however, are very finicky. It is important that you load any box magazine with the cartridge base well back against the rear wall of the magazine.

Regardless of action type, repeaters with box magazines operate by the bolt stripping the cartridge from the magazine and either pushing or carrying it into the chamber. One of the most important facets in this operation is the point at which the cartridge is released from the magazine and comes under the bolt's control. In detachable-magazine rifles this release point is generally controlled by the magazine lips; in non-detachable box magazines it is controlled by the rails at the top of the magazine.

Controlled-round feed actions (Mauser, Springfield, pre-1964 and new Classic Model 70s, Ruger's M77 MK II, etc.) are generally less finicky about the release point—the timing of the rails or magazine lips—than push-feed actions (Remington 700s, post-'64 Model 70s, Savage 110s, Weatherby Mark Vs, etc.). This latter class of action generally works well *as designed and produced by their manufacturers.*

Where I have often run into trouble is when I've rechambered or rebarreled a push-feed bolt-action to a different cartridge case. Being left-handed and faced with a very limited choice of factory chamberings in left-hand models, I've had this done quite a bit. Sometimes the effects are dramatic and startling; I had a Model 700 .300 Winchester Magnum (that started life as a 7mm Remington Magnum) that would hold the cartridges in the magazine just fine—until I started to close the bolt. Then all the cartridges in the magazine would cascade out of the action!

Sometimes the cure is simple. A different follower or a follower spring with different tension may work. For instance, a Remington M700 .375 rebarreled to 8mm Remington Magnum worked like a charm when the Remington follower was replaced with a Ruger M77 follower. Sometimes you can simply bend the magazine lips slightly. Other times the rails must actually be altered. This becomes very difficult and very ticklish work. My recommendation: Cycle a great deal of the proper ammunition through your rifle and make sure there are no hiccups. If there are, don't walk, *run,* to a good gunsmith and get it fixed!

Another critical feeding-related problem is the floorplate dropping open under spring tension and recoil. There are lots of ways to cure this, ranging from stronger springs to, in very extreme cases, welding the darned thing shut. But here's the deal. You do not want your floorplate to drop open and go "bombs away" (or your magazine to drop out) when you're shooting at game. Most rifles that have a propensity to do this will not do it when you load only the chamber, but will do it only when the magazine is fully loaded and under tension of the magazine spring. The cure, again, is a bit of gunsmithing. Discovering the problem, however, requires that you do at least some of your zeroing and practice shooting *with the magazine fully loaded.*

FIRING

Most rifles will fire each and every time the trigger is pulled. The corollary to this is that modern ammunition is so good that ammunition-related misfires are exceedingly rare. You should avoid ammunition of unknown origin like the plague. I trust factory ammunition, and I trust my own handloads. I have a couple of friends whose handloads I also trust—because I've watched them load and know they do it right. My circle of trust extends no farther. If you get a misfire, the first thing you must do is absolutely nothing. Keep the rifle at your shoulder, pointed downrange, and count very slowly to ten. This because a hangfire, or delayed ignition, though rare, is now a possibility. The result can be catastrophic if you've started to open the action!

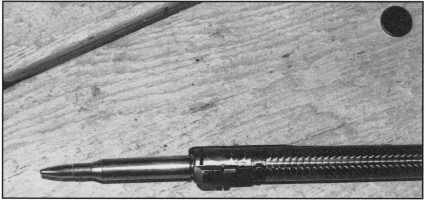

In a controlled-round-feed bolt-action the extractor physically captures the head of the case and traps it against the bolt face.

With controlled-round-feed, like this Dakota Model 76, the rails and spring pressure are not quite as critical as with push-feed actions; the cartridge rises up with the rim slipping between the extractor and the bolt face and then is carried into the chamber.

After counting to ten, keeping the muzzle in a safe direction, slowly open the action and capture the cartridge. The cause could be a bad primer, but modern ammo and components are so good that you should immediately suspect some other cause. Make sure the cartridge is proper for the chamber, and then take a look at the primer. Has it been hit by the firing pin, and has it been hit well, or is there just a slight impression? If the primer shows a good hit, then you *probably* have the rare bad cartridge. Otherwise, you could have a worn or too-short firing pin or a weak spring. Note that different brands of primers differ in hardness of metal and thus in the impression a firing pin will leave. A too-weak strike may look OK in a soft primer, so if this happens again, absolutely go to a gunsmith.

In practice shooting I got several "duds" with that same Belgian-made .416 Rigby. In those days cases were scarce, and I had some with primer pockets that were a bit too deep. I put the problem down to primers seated just a bit out of the firing pin's reach, and I thought that by avoiding those cases I had the problem licked. I got a misfire on an African lion that almost ended in disaster. Eventually, doing what I should have done the first time, I had a gunsmith take a look. There was a metal burr on the striker that would intermittently drag and prevent the firing pin from hitting with enough force!

The other very important part about the firing sequence is that the rifle must fire *only* when the trigger is pulled with the safety off. A nice, light trigger pull is a great aid in accurate shooting, but I am very leery of extremely light triggers. For that matter, I'm very leery of any and all trigger jobs—this is stuff for very competent gunsmiths *only*. It's all too easy to go too far and create a situation where the rifle can fire when the bolt is closed or the rifle is jarred. When examining any unfamiliar rifle, new or used, make certain the gun is empty. With the safety off, work the action very hard and fast a number of times—making absolutely certain your fingers are well away from the trigger. If the hammer falls just once, yes, it's gunsmith time again. Carry this a step farther and, again being absolutely certain the rifle is empty, cock the action and, keeping the muzzle in a safe direction, hold the rifle by the barrel and rap the butt smartly on the floor. Again, if the hammer falls just once, you've got a big problem.

So long as the firing mechanism hasn't been altered by incompetent hands, a "jar-off" or discharge on closing the action should never happen. However, if it should, you *must* take the rifle to a very good gunsmith immediately. Just last fall, in Colorado, I had a hunter's rifle fire when he closed the bolt. The rifle was very close to my ear at the time, and the detonation (from a .300 Weatherby with a muzzle brake!) flattened me. Needless to say, I was mad as hell—but I was angrier when my hunter admitted that the rifle had done this before! The rifle was a Weatherby Mark V, but it wasn't Weatherby's problem. The factory trigger had been replaced, but the new trigger was a good brand—

it wasn't their fault, either. Now, the ham-handed idiot who did the trigger work—that's the guy I'd like to get *my* mitts on!

EXTRACTION

Extraction—pulling the case out of the chamber, whether fired or unfired—is generally a very simple matter: It works or it doesn't. On older rifles you can occasionally run into worn extractors, but extraction problems are *usually* ammunition-related. A bolt-action has the strongest camming power and the greatest leverage for pulling cases out of the chamber; all the other action types are more finicky in this regard. If there's a problem, it usually results from a cartridge that either has a bad case or develops enough pressure so that it expands beyond the extractor's power to remove it.

There should not be a problem with standard factory ammunition. However, some factories—Norma and Weatherby, for instance—do load their ammo a bit "warmer" than most U.S.

With push-feed actions, timing of the rails and magazine spring pressure are all-important; the cartridge must be released from the magazine in just the right position to enable the bolt to push it the rest of the way into the chamber. Push-feeds work very well as manufactured, but can be very finicky if rebarreled or rechambered to a different cartridge.

The tendency at the range is to feed cartridges directly into the chamber. That's OK some of the time, but make sure you do some shooting with a full magazine, and cycle every cartridge you are taking hunting from the magazine into the chamber. This little litmus test will uncover most potential problems.

manufacturers. The new "hot" loads—Federal's High Energy and Hornady's Light Magnum and Heavy Magnum lines—are also loaded to higher pressures. Some rifles, especially levers, pumps, and semiautos, can balk at extracting these loads. The problem is much more likely with handloads, especially if you're loading to "near maximum." I had a Savage 99 in .308 that froze up hopelessly when I fired one of my handloads in Africa. My fault altogether; I didn't think the loads were that hot, but I was wrong!

Just to avoid potential problems, it's best to back off a bit from max when handloading for hunting. The other thing is that you must not let your ammunition get hot. Ammunition increases in pressure as temperatures rise. This is not normally significant enough to cause problems if ammunition is kept in the shade. However, if you leave a box of shells on the dashboard on a sunny day, you can get into trouble. Likewise, if you develop your handloads in the States at 30 degrees, then go hunting in Mexico or Africa at 90 degrees, you're dealing with altogether different pressures. This will *normally* not be a problem with factory loads, but if you've handloaded to near maximum you may run into sticky extraction. I suspect this was my problem with that Savage 99.

Other than bad ammo or a worn extractor, the other potential problem is debris or dirt that gets caught between the extractor and the bolt face. I'm not a real stickler for constant gun cleaning, but I have had this problem a couple of times. Taking a look at the extractor groove should be part of routine inspection, especially if you're hunting under dirty, dusty, or sandy conditions, or if you're dragging your rifle through lots of brush.

EJECTION

As a handloader, I don't really want my rifles to throw their cases twenty feet into the brush. But while you're on the range, whether actually firing or merely cycling your ammo through the rifle, make absolutely certain that the cases are actually ejecting. This is easy to miss, since on the range many of us—especially we handloaders—tend to open our actions daintily and pluck the cases from the chamber. That's fine most of the time, but make certain you fully cycle the action a number of times to ensure that it really is ejecting.

Mauser-type rifles (Dakota, Model 70, Springfield, etc.) usually have fixed-blade ejectors in the rear of the action that operate through a slot in the bolt face. These can become worn, but it's a very simple and inexpensive repair to replace them. Some years ago I got a great deal on a Mauser-actioned Westley Richards .318. This fine rifle has a cartridge firing a .330-inch bullet, but it's pretty obscure today. I found some old Kynoch ammo, plus I made some cases by shortening and necking up .30-06 cases. Needless to say, I didn't want to lose any of those cases, so I was carefully plucking them from the chamber. I shot it quite a few times before I realized that it wasn't ejecting at all! The late Jack Lott, a wonderful gunsmith as well as a real expert on heavy rifles,

In the case of dangerous game, mechanical problems may cost you a whole lot more than a lost opportunity at a great trophy. Leave as little to chance as possible, and start well ahead of your departure date. Murphy was right—whatever can go wrong will. Especially if you wait until the last minute.

was with me at the range that day. Wonder of wonders, he had a Mauser ejector somewhere in his kit, and we fixed it on the spot!

Most push-feed actions with enclosed bolt faces have a spring-loaded ejector in the bolt face. It's very rare for them to wear out, but dirt and gunk can retard their action. If your rifle is sluggish in ejection, try cleaning the bolt with a good degreaser and then relubricating lightly. If this doesn't work, see a gunsmith. Although a bit more complex than a Mauser, this is still a very simple repair.

MECHANICAL SAFETY

I don't trust safeties. A mechanical safety is no substitute for proper gun handling. I don't carry a slung rifle with a round in the chamber, and of course I don't carry rifles in vehicles or saddle scabbards with rounds in the chamber. The only time a rifle should have a round in the chamber is when you're on your feet, with the rifle firmly under control, and you're expecting a shot at any time. Needless to say, the muzzle should be kept in a safe direction at all times. I see the mechanical safety as a backup system should you stumble or fall under such circumstances.

That said, it simply must work. As you become familiar with a new (or used) rifle, run the same kinds of tests that I discussed under "Firing." Making absolutely certain the rifle is unloaded and keeping the muzzle in a safe direction, make certain the hammer will not fall when the safety is engaged. Then, with the safety engaged (and with the muzzle still pointed in a safe direction), rap the butt on a hard floor a few times. If the hammer or striker *ever* falls with the safety engaged, just once, get the rifle to a gunsmith immediately.

The other thing about safeties is that they should not be all that easy to take on and off. You don't want to grunt and strain and hurt your thumb or finger when moving them from "safe" to "fire" and vice versa, but you want enough tension so that the safety lever or knob can't be easily brushed into the fire position. If it moves mushily or too easily, a stronger spring or a new part will usually fix the problem.

I'm not real picky about the placement of a mechanical safety, so long as it's accessible and it works, and I'm not hard-over on three-position safeties. Again, the safety is no substitute for proper gun handling; if you're unloading a rifle by cycling the action, that muzzle simply must be pointed in a safe direction whether the safety is engaged or not. On bolt-actions, however, I much prefer a safety that also locks the bolt. When I'm carrying a bolt-action slung over my back or shoulder, out of sight and out of control, the chamber will be empty—but I much prefer that the bolt also be locked down by the safety. All too often, on rifles that lacked this feature, I've grabbed the rifle and found that brush or my movement had opened the bolt, allowing snow, dirt, or twigs to get down in the action and magazine.

Again, mechanical problems of any type are rare with factory rifles in unaltered condition, but they can and do occur. Those long summer days at the range are the time to discover them and get them fixed, not the day before opening day or, worse, when the buck of your dreams steps out of the brush!

CHAPTER TWELVE

KEEPING IT CLEAN

A hunting buddy of mine, Lad Shunneson, absolutely swears by his Browning BAR semiauto. This battered .300 Winchester Magnum is probably the most-traveled BAR in existence. Lad has carried it to literally all the continents on Earth, and during the couple of decades he has owned it the rifle has taken a prodigious quantity of game. This is relatively unusual; Lad is one of few international hunters who relies almost exclusively on a self-loader. He's run into a few countries that wouldn't allow him to bring it in, but all in all the rifle has provided exceptionally good service. It works for him.

What is truly unusual is the fact that Lad simply doesn't believe in cleaning rifles. In fact, he absolutely swears that his Browning semiauto has *never* been cleaned. From its appearance I believe him! He throws on a bit of lubricant from time to time, but he has never cleaned the bore and the action has never been stripped down. I do not offer this as a model for the way you should treat your firearms, but rather as a testament to how durable and reliable well-made modern firearms really are!

I must admit that I'm not a stickler for cleaning rifles every time they're uncased. I have friends who are, and I admire their fastidiousness. Necessity probably lies somewhere between the compulsion to clean a rifle every time it's fired and my buddy Lad's reactionary insistence on never cleaning. There are, of

Although there are some exotic and even electronic gun-cleaning methods, doing the old-fashioned way you learned from your Dad works just fine. Get the rifle in a steady rest, and if you possibly can, clean from the breech, not from the muzzle.

There is a plethora of fine gun-cleaning products on the market. Always read the directions; some products are better on powder residue than metal fouling, and some are strong enough that they should not be left in the barrel for extended periods.

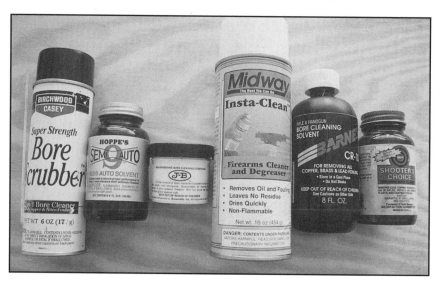

course, several levels of rifle cleaning. One level is merely wiping down the outside metal surfaces when you put a rifle away or when you're done for the day. Unless your rifle sports a genuine rustproof finish, this should always be done. Fingerprints are one of the worst rust-producing agents, and are particularly bad on blued steel. Yet another level involves taking the rifle out of the stock and getting all the gunk and moisture off the hidden metal surfaces and out of the nooks and crannies. And then there's bore cleaning. Similarly, this can range from simply "punching the bore" with a lubricated patch to prevent rust, all the way to detailed cleaning intended to remove all fouling. How often you should clean, and what level of cleaning is really essential, depends on the conditions the rifle is used under, the ammunition, and also the individual barrel.

In wet or humid weather, or in coastal climates, rust can get ahead of you very quickly. On my forest safaris in Central Africa, for instance, not only was the climate very hot and humid, but there was at least some rain—sometimes real gullywashers—every couple of days. Daily cleaning was absolutely essential, and even then it was impossible to stay completely ahead of rust. Here I mean *cleaning*. On my first forest hunt I took a much-battered Winchester Model 70. I wiped it down carefully and punched the bore every day, but did little else. On my second forest hunt I took a new John Rigby .416, a valuable rifle that was my new pride and joy. I not only wiped it down and punched the bore; I took the action out of the stock for cleaning, and I rubbed in good stock oil every day. Despite all the care I could lavish, the rifle was a wreck after three weeks in the forest. The lesson is probably twofold: Very rough conditions are what synthetic stocks, stainless steel, and rustproof coatings are all about. If you prefer the traditional look and feel of good wood and blued steel, don't cry about the wear and tear!

Under more normal conditions, a quick wipedown with a silicone cloth will keep most rust at bay. In sandy or dusty country, taking an old toothbrush into the nooks and crannies may become part of a daily routine. You must let the climate tell you what is required to ensure that your rifle keeps working as it should.

This applies to cleaning the barrel as well, but cleaning the bore is a different and somewhat more complex issue. Here is where the ammunition used and a barrel's individuality come into play. Virtually all centerfire ammunition manufactured today uses non-corrosive priming and propellants. Needless to say, this does not apply to blackpowder or Pyrodex. Both are quite corrosive, Pyrodex only slightly less so than the good old smelly stuff. If you're shooting a muzzleloader or a blackpowder cartridge gun, you'd best clean the bore thoroughly within a few hours of firing it. Although it's getting scarce today, there's still some older ammo around that has corrosive priming. This is not all military ammo. In a previous chapter I mentioned a Westley Richards .318 I used to have. Most of the original ammo I obtained for this rifle was corrosive primed, likewise some of the old fodder for double rifles that is still around. There are many good solvents that will work, but one of the best answers for blackpowder, Pyrodex, and corrosive priming is to pour boiling water down the bore. Then you can clean and lubricate just like anything else.

Corrosive components, however, are not the only ammunition-related cleaning problem. Virtually all bullets leave some residue in the barrel that will eventually build up, but some are much worse than others. If you shoot cast lead bullets a lot, you know that lead fouling is a problem. Copper fouling is also a problem. This is not extremely pronounced with most bullet jackets of copper alloy, but pure copper can foul terribly. As much as I admire the performance of Barnes X-Bullets on game, the X is one bullet that is bad about leaving copper residue in a barrel.

What fouling means depends on the individual barrel. Some barrels are very smooth and resist fouling quite well; other barrels are rougher and gather fouling very quickly. You can look in the muzzle of one barrel and see the bright green of heavy copper fouling, but that barrel may continue to shoot very well. The accuracy of another barrel may deteriorate rapidly with the first hint of fouling. Ultimately your rifle must tell you how clean it must be to shoot its best.

If you're one of those guys who cleans thoroughly every time you go shooting, you will never discover this . . . and perhaps that's just as well. But if you're not a stickler for gun cleaning, you will discover that sooner or later your groups will deteriorate for no apparent reason. Chances are it's time to clean the bore! I have a couple of rifles that simply must be cleaned every twenty or thirty shots or I can see the difference in the group size, while I have others that are far more forgiving. The little .17 Remington is famous for fouling, and many of them need to be thoroughly cleaned as often as every dozen shots. Every rifle is different, but there are very few like Lad's BAR that give good service year in and year out with no maintenance!

Gun cleaning is not particularly complex, but it can be time-consuming—especially if you have a serious buildup of fouling to remove. Perhaps this is an excuse based on laziness, but I don't think constant cleaning is any better for a barrel than never cleaning. I do think *periodic* cleaning is far better than letting the fouling build up until it takes forever to get it out. One argument in my favor, and something to keep in mind: The first bullet from a freshly cleaned barrel is almost certain to land in a different spot than subsequent bullets. I won't try to explain this; it's one of the idiosyncraies of riflery. But put it in the bank. The difference varies with the rifle; it can be an insignificant fraction of an inch, or it can be a couple of inches. Serious accuracy buffs *always* fire a "fouling shot" or two before firing for "group and score." If I "detail clean" a barrel, I don't do it right before a hunt. Instead, I do it just before a final sight-in session, and then I don't intend to clean the barrel until after I return. Obviously this doesn't always work. If your rifle is subjected to a lot of dust or moisture, you have to at least "wipe down" the inside of your barrel along with the outer metal—but if you leave lubricant inside the barrel you will probably change your first-round point of impact significantly.

There are a few basic bore-cleaning rules. Whenever possible, clean *from the breech*. This is because a slip with a cleaning rod or jag can mar the rifling, and the muzzle area is exactly where you don't want this to happen. With slides, levers, and semiautos you generally have little choice but to clean from the muzzle, and this is OK—but you must be very careful as you fit the jag into the muzzle and push the rod through.

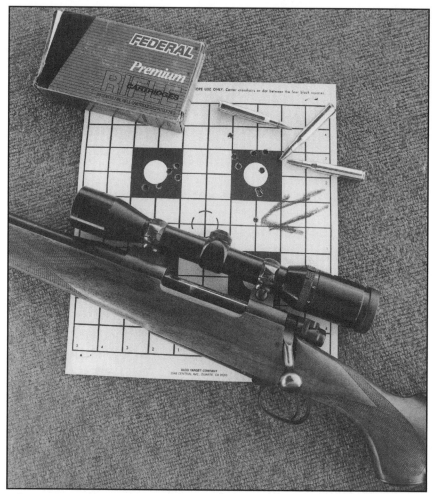

There isn't a particularly good group on this target, but the significant point is the one shot marked with an arrow. This was the first "fouling" shot from a clean barrel, and it went to an altogether different place from the rest. This is not uncommon.

I'm cleaning my .416 Rigby in a forest camp in Central Africa. Jungle climate is very hard on firearms; despite daily cleaning I was unable to stay ahead of the rust.

Cleaning a bore is really no different today than it was when your dad (or the military) taught you how to do it. You loosen the fouling with a solvent-soaked brush, and then you wipe it out with successive cotton patches (the flannel patches you buy are great, but patches cut from old T-shirts work just as well) until they come out clean. This is the "good old way" to clean a bore, and it works just fine. However, it works much better if you use solvents designed to clean your particular type of fouling.

With today's rampant environmental concerns, some of the tried-and-true solvent recipes have been watered down considerably and are no longer the cure-all they used to be. In particular, most commercial bore cleaners are very good for powder fouling but not so good for metal fouling. If copper fouling is your problem, you need a bore cleaner with a very high ammonia content. I use Barnes's CR-10 copper solvent, which the company developed to cure the serious copper fouling of its own X-Bullet. Shooter's Choice works well also. In fact, both work so well that you probably don't want to leave them in the bore for extended periods of time! You also must not use a copper solvent with the typical brass or copper bore brush; the stuff will eat it just like it eats bore fouling! I usually apply it with a nylon brush, then let it sit in the bore for about twenty minutes. Then I get it all out, eventually using a conventional non-ammoniac bore cleaner.

With virtually all bore cleaners and bore-cleaning techniques you simply must read the directions, as unmanly as it seems, and follow them. The folks who designed the products do have some idea of how best to utilize them. Often, however, it won't be quite as easy as the directions suggest. If you have a serious buildup of fouling (or a particularly rough bore) you may have to repeat the cleaning sequence a number of times.

Most commercial bore cleaners work well, especially if serious metal fouling is not present. I like good old J-B Bore Cleaner, a paste that is actually a very mild abrasive. A standby of benchrest shooters for years, it is one of the best products for periodic bore cleaning. A new product designed by Greg Warne (formerly of Kimber) is called simply, "The World's Fastest Gun Bore Cleaner." It consists of a weight and a pull-through cord followed by a caliber-sized flossing rope with *embedded* multiple copper brushes. Just soak the rope in the solvent of your choice and pull it through a few times. It works, and when it gets too gunky you can wash it. This is a very simple tool. Much more complex are the electric "rods" that, when left in your barrel and plugged in, use electromagnetic energy to literally pull the fouling from your barrel and plate it onto the rod. I must admit that I have never actually used this cleaning technique—it's a bit too high-tech for my tastes. However, a number of my friends have purchased this setup and it works amazingly well.

Most gunshops offer a bewildering array of cleaning products. Equally good sources are the major catalogs like Cabela's, Midway Arms, and Brownell's. You need to establish your own cleaning routine designed to prevent rust and similar damage, and also to maintain accuracy. I can't tell you exactly what to use or how often you must perform the ritual—but I don't recommend you treat your rifle like my buddy Lad does his old BAR. Given such treatment, most rifles will eventually go on strike!

═══ CHAPTER THIRTEEN ═══

TROUBLESHOOTING ACCURACY

It's relatively easy to come up with a cookbook for improving accuracy: First you follow Step A, then Step B, Step C, and so on—and you can watch your groups shrink as you progress. Unfortunately it usually doesn't work quite that way. As has been stressed throughout this volume, rifles are individuals. Some fall into line quite readily, some are recalcitrant, and some are downright antisocial. There *is* a "cookbook" for accuracy, and it progresses from the simplest adjustments to the most complex. This is because the fix may be simple, so there's no point in doing something complex. The dilemma is that you never know exactly what might work on a given rifle . . . and after all of your efforts, it's also possible that *nothing* will work.

As we've seen in previous chapters, you may be stuck with a bad barrel. This one is relatively easy to figure out. You can't make a silk purse out of a sow's ear. If you've tried the simple fixes and you're still getting groups that look more like shotgun patterns, chances are you're wasting your time by going to the more time-consuming and/or expensive solutions. Under such circumstances, if the accuracy you're getting isn't something you can live with, you're better off to choke it up and invest in a new barrel.

On the other hand, some rifles will tantalize you endlessly by being almost there. Often this is a matter of unrealistic expectations or, put another way, the "delta" between the accuracy you want and the accuracy you're getting. Part of this is my fault, mine and at least my generation of gunwriters—if not the previous couple of generations as well. For years we have written matter-of-factly about sub-one-inch groups, so much so that such accuracy is expected as a matter of course. I'm certainly not suggesting such groups are not real, but in the way that all humans are prone to exaggerate a bit, it's easy to "throw out" the flyers, or take the best group and forget all the rest. Many out-of-the-box sporting rifles manufactured today will indeed shoot half-inch groups. But many will not, and most that will can perform to that level only with carefully selected ammo and perfect conditions.

Efforts to improve accuracy should always take into consideration the level of accuracy you really need . . . and what you can reasonably hope to attain. These are normal groups from my Mark Bansner 7x57, which has a very light barrel. It's sort of an "inch and a quarter" rifle—and I consider it both accurate and, more importantly, accurate enough.

Not too long ago I got a letter from a frustrated reader. He had a custom .30-06, and now it was on its third barrel. Despite repeated rebedding and rebarreling, all he could get out of the rifle was groups averaging just under an inch. Folks, that ain't bad! The .30-06 is a fine cartridge, but it rarely produces benchrest accuracy. As I recall, he was using a military controlled-round-feed action, which is wonderful for reliability but generally not as accurate as a push-feed action like a Remington 700 or Savage 110. He was also using standard-quality barrels, not "match grade" or specially selected barrels. I have written elsewhere about some very accurate rifles that I own. My Rogue River 8mm, for instance, is a quarter-inch rifle on a bad day—but it wears a best-quality Pac-Nor barrel. My David Miller 7mm Remington Magnum is almost as accurate—but it wears a Krieger match-grade barrel. My Kenny Jarrett .30-06 is the rare sub-half-inch .30-06, but Jarrett made the barrel himself. If you're really serious about braggin'-size groups, the best course is to start with a barrel *made* to produce such groups—but understand that such a barrel will cost three or four times as much as a good replacement barrel.

With that in mind, it's worthwhile considering how much accuracy you *need*, not necessarily how much you *want*. I submit that the gentleman who owns a .30-06 that will *consistently* deliver one-inch groups has a rifle that will do absolutely everything a .30-06 should be asked to do! Teeny-tiny groups are great for impressing your friends, but not all rifles will produce them, and you don't have to have them for effective big-game hunting under most circumstances. If you want a serious long-range rig, that's different. You need serious accuracy. Likewise if we're talking a varmint rifle versus a big-game rifle. For most big-game hunting, consistent $1^{1}/_{2}$-inch groups are good enough. Most rifles—including all the action types—will at least do this if you follow the "recipe."

Many, especially the bolt-actions, will do much better . . . but there's no guarantee. This, by the way, is not a caveat against failure. It's just fact. Several of my personal favorite hunting rifles have been "inch-and-a-quarter to inch-and-a-half" rifles, and I've never apologized for them. I had a fiberglass-stocked .338 that Chet Brown put together for me. It handled like a dream, and I shot a great deal of game with it—but I don't think I ever got an *honest* one-inch group out of it. The .375 H&H, big though it is, can be a wonderfully accurate cartridge. My old left-hand-converted pre-'64—with which I've taken not only a number of Cape buffalo but also a wide variety of plains game at varying ranges—was rarely better than an "inch-and-a-half" gun. I eventually shot the barrel out and replaced it. Now it does better—but it was always good enough. Don't get me wrong; accuracy builds confidence, and is always worth striving for . . . but don't give up on a good rifle because it doesn't deliver the accuracy someone said you should have. The only person it has to be good enough for is *you*.

These were some of the "initial inventory" groups with our two "project rifles," both in .30-06—a Model 700 ADL in wooden stock (top rifle, left target); and a Model 700 synthetic stock (bottom rifle, right target). Some groups are mediocre and some are quite good, indicating excellent potential.

A close look at one of the first targets fired with the synthetic-stocked Model 700 revealed a group of very close to a half-inch with Remington Extended Range factory ammo. With groups like this from an out-of-the-box rifle with factory ammo, topped with an average hunting scope, there's no reason to proceed further with this rifle.

OK, let's start with our cookbook. We'll assume you have a rifle you want to group a bit better than it does. In an earlier chapter we talked about bedding. This is not the first thing you want to mess with, not at all. But start with a visual inspection. If you can actually *see* stock material bearing on one side of the barrel and not the other, chances are you have a problem. This will usually manifest itself in horizontal group dispersion; it should be obvious that the pressure must be relieved.

Gross bedding problems like this are not common. But let's continue with a visual inspection. Check all of your screws. A loose action screw or, in a two-piece stock, a loose fore-end is often the culprit. Make sure they're good and tight. If you determine a propensity for the screws to loosen, Loc-Tite them in! With all the screws tight, put pressure on the barrel in several directions and make sure the action isn't

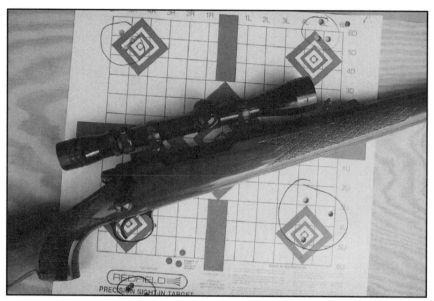

The wooden-stocked ADL, a used rifle with unknown history, didn't produce any really spectacular groups at first, but its average was actually a bit better than the new synthetic-stocked rifle. This suggests some improvement is very likely.

wobbling. If you've got movement, you have little chance for accuracy.

Check your scope mount and all of the ring screws and make certain everything is tight. Now, if everything is tight and there's no apparent gross bedding problem, you've got a more difficult situation. Maybe. The next thing to check is your shooting technique. To determine a rifle's raw accuracy, the idea is to remove as much of the human element as possible. You want to use a very solid benchrest, and sandbag the rifle as solidly as possible. If the rifle kicks you, wear a P.A.S.T. recoil shield or put a towel (or even a sandbag) between your shoulder and the rifle. Pay attention to how you set the fore-end onto the rest or sandbags. Rest it well back from the fore-end tip, do not rest on the sling swivel stud, and put the fore-end on the rest in the same place every time. Put another sandbag under the butt, and adjust the height so that the sights are centered on the target with no movement whatsoever. The best technique is to use your supporting hand to pull the butt back into your shoulder, *not* touching the fore-end. Make sure your barrel is cool and at least reasonably clean. Take a deep breath, let part of it out, and concentrate on sight alignment and trigger squeeze.

If you're doing all of this, and you have good ammo, then the rifle should be delivering something close to what it is capable of. At this stage, beyond radical fixes like remanufacturing the rifle (truing the action) or changing the barrel, you have two main areas to look at: The ammo may be good, but it may not be what your rifle likes; or the bedding also may be just fine, but it may not be what your barrel needs to shoot its best. Part of bedding, by the way, is pressure on the barrel. The bedding itself may be just fine, but there may be too much or too little pressure on the barrel.

You can always play with different loads, but before you mess with the bedding there's one more thing you should check. This is rare, but it's always possible for internal components in your scope to shift.

My 8mm Remington Magnum was a classic case. We had a very good barrel, and it was bedded with loving care. The chamber was well cut, and the action was true. Geoff Miller, the ultimate accuracy freak, loaded the ammo with Sierra bullets with painstaking precision. The rifle was a disappointment. It shot OK—maybe an inch, maybe a bit less, but nothing like we thought it should. Mind you, we might have accepted that, except we knew that everything was put together better than that. So we tried everything. A bit more pressure on the fore-end. Up a half-grain, down a half-grain. Well, it was hunting season and the rifle certainly shot well enough.

I took it to North Carolina and shot a huge black bear with it, and then we went out to cull some white-tailed does. I missed one clean at about three hundred yards. Then I missed another at about 150 yards, and then hit it in the neck with the second

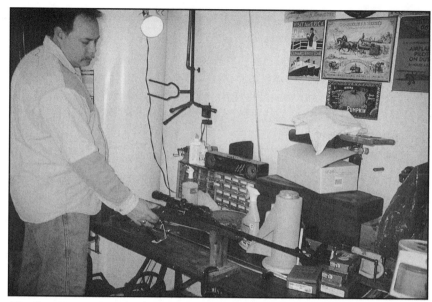

The first step was to give the ADL a thorough cleaning. That's Geoff Miller on the cleaning rod, cleaning from the breech and using a bore guide. The rifle had apparently been carried (or stored) much and shot little; there was little fouling, and initial groups after cleaning didn't change much.

shot. Except I was aiming at the shoulder. We put the rifle on paper, and the scope had shifted. Hmmm. When I got it back home it had shifted yet again. I switched the offending scope for a 4.5-14X Leupold that was on another rifle, and that 8mm hasn't looked back. Just last weekend fellow lefty Dave Petzal, of *Field & Stream*, shot a ¼-inch group with it. That's a good group, but not one of its better ones! In his defense, the benchrest wasn't very steady. . . .

If everything else seems right, the cheapest thing you can do is switch a scope from a rifle of known accuracy, if only for a couple of groups. The trick to finding what works is simply to isolate *all* the variables, and there are many to isolate.

In later chapters we'll talk about selecting factory loads, and also handloading for hunting. Here it's essential to point out that there is no predicting exactly which loads will shoot best in a given rifle. In most cases a few loads shoot horribly and a few shoot very well, with most somewhere in between. This is normal. If you have a rifle that shoots several loads reasonably well, then there is a good chance you can improve things dramatically. We'll get to that. If you have a rifle that doesn't seem to shoot *anything* very well, then you may have a hopeless case. But not always!

I had an over-the-counter Remington Mountain Rifle in a Kevlar stock, chambered to .280 Remington. As mentioned earlier, this is largely a handloader's cartridge. It was even more so back then; Norma had a factory load, and Remington had two or three flavors. The Remington .280 factory loads are pretty good, and I've gotten some decent groups out of them with several rifles. But not this one! With Remington factory ammo, that rifle—with Swarovski scope—produced groups of about six inches. No kidding! The Norma ammo grouped well enough to hunt with, but just barely. I tried a very standard

Next step was to check all the screws for tightness. This was not a problem, and there seemed to be no shifting of the rifle in the stock.

handload of 55 grains of H4831 behind 150-grain Nosler Ballistic Tips, and the groups shrank to one inch. Instantly!

However, the best "finicky gun" story I know belongs to Geoff Miller, who assisted me immeasurably in the technical aspects of this book. Many, many years ago he saw a Remington Model 721 in .300 H&H in a gunshop. He had to have it, and he bought it. The rifle had a long barrel of medium contour, and with good loads the old H&H is a very accurate cartridge. Except this one wouldn't shoot. At all. He played with the bedding and the loads, but it seemed hopeless. One day, he gave up on it. He was firing Sierra Match Kings behind a reasonably full charge of 4831, and he had shimmed the fore-end with one thickness of matchbook cover. He fired one round, and it landed right where it should. He fired again, and the target was clean. He fired again, and there was still just one hole in the target. In the exasperation of youth, he grabbed the rifle by the barrel and hurled it into a snowbank. Except he didn't let go in time, and the front sight cut his forefinger to the bone.

Bleeding profusely and swearing even more so he stalked down to collect his target. Instead of one hole, it showed three bullet holes touching in a perfect cloverleaf. Ignoring the blood on the snow, he dug down and found the rifle. With that load, and only that load—and one matchbook cover shim—he won benchrest matches, and a couple of years later took the rifle with him to Vietnam for other shooting matches. He still has it, and I've seen him cut the links off a hanging chain, one by one, at two hundred yards with his "Death Ray." But after forty years he still can't vary the load by a half-grain—and that matchbook shim, soaked in oil, is still in place!

Both of these rifles, my .280 and Geoff's .300, are unique in that they're at the outer limits of finickiness. My .280 would *never* shoot factory loads even marginally well, but so long as I used slow-burning powders it responded pretty well to handloads with most bullets from 140 to 160 grains. Geoff's .300 is even

With all the external factors checked out, the rifle seemed to exhibit some horizontal stringing in the groups. We removed the action from the wood and, with a round file, smoothed out the barrel channel. The rifle was pressure-bedded with a large "pad" at the fore-end tip—but it appeared uneven and may have created too much pressure.

more finicky; after a great deal of effort, the only difference between superb performance and nonperformance was a very slight variance in powder charge. This can happen, and this is why you must be exhaustive in your search for the right ammo if you care about maximum accuracy. Fortunately this degree of difficulty is unusual. Many rifles will shoot terribly with a few loads and wonderfully with a few others, but will be reasonably consistent with *most* loads.

Don't forget, too, that some rifles are very finicky about bullet weights. Just recently I was testing one of the new Beretta Mato synthetic-stocked bolt-actions. I was going elk hunting with the rifle, and I wanted to use 250-grain bullets. Unfortunately this rifle didn't want to shoot 250-grain bullets. The groups were two inches and more, simply horrible for a new bolt-action today. I called my contact at Beretta, and he insisted this rifle was a real shooter. Turns out he was right, but only with lighter bullets. Groups shrank to just over an inch with Hornady Heavy Magnum 225-grain factory loads, and I'm sure it would have done even better with good handloads.

Provided you haven't detected a gross bedding problem, I think the wisest course is to work with a variety of ammo *before* you mess with the bedding. There are several reasons for this. First, whether factory or handload, you may pick one of those loads that your rifle doesn't like, so you have a poor representation of your rifle's accuracy. You may be messing with perfectly good bedding when all you needed to do was switch ammo. Second, no matter what you do it's unlikely that you can achieve dramatic results. Gains in the accuracy game are generally incremental, not radical—and it's just as possible to change things for the worse as for the better. Before you start to change anything in the rifle's structure, you need to go through all the external factors.

Then you need to be reasonable in your expectations, and this may include a decision as to whether or not further effort is worth it. If you've tightened everything, checked everything, and gone through an exhaustive ammo search, and you're still getting three-inch groups, there isn't much point in going to a lot of trouble with the bedding. On the other hand, if you've got a rifle that groups $1^1/_2$ inches or so with at least some loads, then it probably wants to shoot and needs a bit of help. Mind you, the chances are very slim that you can turn such a rifle into a tackdriver, but you might get it down to an inch or so. Similarly, if your groups hover around an inch with good ammo that the rifle likes, you may be able to get it down a bit, but you probably can't turn it into a benchrest gun. Again, improvement is incremental, not exponential. There is also a point at which you should leave well enough alone, but you'll have to be the judge of that.

Let's turn now to our two project rifles. The first one, the new synthetic-stocked Remington 700, was all too easy. Some loads it didn't like. It didn't like the Lapua 180-grain factory load, which is a very good and normally accurate load. It didn't

After a bit of smoothing the stringing went from vertical to horizontal, still indicating too much pressure on the barrel. We checked the recoil lug screw, and it was very tight. Geoff Miller backed off on the pressure just a bit—and the result was dramatic.

like Federal's High Energy load with 180-grain Nosler Partitions. It did a bit better with Speer Nitrex, but not great. It did a bit better with some of my "standard" handloads, but not great. Then I tried Remington 178-grain Extended Range, and the rifle shot a group measuring .450-inch. At this point we were finished. There is a good possibility that I can improve on this performance, but I'll have to do it with ammo. I'm not going to mess with a straight out-of-the-box .30-06 that can shoot sub-half-inch groups with factory ammunition. Not me!

The wooden-stocked ADL was actually more interesting. This rifle had a fair amount of surface rust, showing a lot of handling and poor care, but I doubt it had been shot a great deal. Across the spectrum of the same ammunition, it actually delivered better *average* groups than the synthetic-stocked rifle. There were a couple of loads that it didn't like, but it turned in solid $1\frac{1}{4}$-inch groups with several. Federal Premium High Energy 165-grain Trophy Bonded hovered right at an inch, and, coincidentally, the best group came with the same Remington Extended Range 178-grain ammo. That group was right at $\frac{7}{8}$-inch. This rifle wanted to shoot. And this level of performance is ideal for attempting improvement.

I'm neither an accuracy freak nor a good technician; patience is not my long suit. So I enlisted Geoff Miller's help in seeing what could be done with this rifle. Miller, proprietor of Rogue River Rifleworks and John Rigby & Co., Gunmakers, Ltd. in Paso Robles, California, is one of the finickiest accuracy freaks I've ever met. He has the patience and the know-how, and has held benchrest world records in his day.

The first step was a serious cleaning . . . something this rifle hadn't seen for quite a spell. However, the barrel was just dirty, not grossly fouled. Our suspicion that it had been handled a whole lot more than shot seemed to be correct. And since serious metal fouling was not in evidence, we weren't surprised when accuracy stayed the same after cleaning. We fired several more groups with factory ammo, this time firing five-shot groups versus three-shot groups. The difference in group size was negligible, but this time we noticed evidence of vertical stringing.

At this stage we took some things on blind faith, such as the chamber being straight and the action/barrel mating being reasonably true. While such things can be measured, fixing them gets expensive. Besides, the accuracy was good enough to suggest no serious problems. Further, our goal was to maximize the potential of a good hunting rifle, not create a benchrest gun.

The Remington Model 700 has a forward action screw that goes into a recoil lug. It was good and tight . . . but just maybe it was too tight. Holding the barrel, we moved the screw back and forth, and could actually feel the barrel move. Perhaps there was too much pressure. We backed off the screw, and the vertical stringing changed to horizontal stringing!

Now, finally, it was time to play with the bedding. We took the action out of the stock to see what we had. The action inletting looked pretty good, and we already knew that there was no apparent shifting. So we turned to the barrel channel. It showed some high spots that could potentially put pressure on the barrel, and there was a thick pad about two inches back from the fore-end tip, creating the pressure-bedding situation we discussed in an earlier chapter.

Geoff Miller is a great believer in pressure-bedding, and he has made a believer of me. However, there is such a thing as too much of a good thing. Working with a round file, he

Never believe just one group. These two additional five-shot groups, one fired by Geoff Miller and one by me, are virtually identical. They show five shots in 1 inches—on a gusty, blustery day—and each had three shots in less than ³/₄ inch. This is with factory loads. It doesn't get much better than this on a consistent basis.

removed the high spots in the barrel channel and reduced the "pressure pad" quite a bit. Then we went back to the bench.

With the barrel channel smoothed and a bit of pressure relieved, this time the horizontal *and* vertical stringing were gone. We did not achieve sub-half-inch groups, but now the rifle was firing nice round clusters. Three-shot groups with Remington Extended Range—which the rifle still seemed to like—averaged just over a half-inch, and five-shot groups stayed right at an inch—consistently. This, by the way, was on a gusty day, far from ideal. Perhaps we could do a bit better on a better day, and almost certainly we could do better by tailoring handloads to the rifle. But, after all, "good enough is good enough." We now had an "off-the-used-gun-rack" .30-06, mounted with a twenty-year-old used scope, that delivered *consistent* minute-of-angle groups with factory ammunition.

I expected to try the "business card shim" trick on this rifle, but it turned out to have plenty of upward pressure—initially too much—built into the factory bedding. This rifle, then, was "fixed" with different screw pressure and less than ten minutes of work with a round file. Every rifle is different, but the normal range for dampening vibration and making it consistent is 5 to 7 pounds of upward pressure, usually applied about an inch back from the fore-end tip. A normal business card is about .015-inch thick, but there is no formula for how many it takes to exert enough pressure. That depends entirely on the barrel channel and the barrel. A stock that has been free-floated may require several thicknesses of business cards to take up the slack and exert upward pressure; a stock that has been tightly contact-bedded may need just one. The other thing to keep in mind is that this may improve accuracy, it may make no difference, and it may make it worse; there is no panacea for accuracy, but screw tension and upward pressure are the easiest experiments . . . and it's amazing how often these will create measurable improvement.

Here let me give you a caution: Never, ever believe anything you learn from one or two groups. If you're a very good benchrest shooter and the conditions are ideal, you *may* learn something, but there are good flukes and bad flukes, and the only things that matter are repetition and averages. Especially when you're talking about hunting rifles, rather than benchrest rifles or varmint rifles, three-shot groups are fine . . . but you need to shoot *more* three-shot groups to have the same statistical validity you get from five-shot groups. It is also easier to shoot three-shot groups. So that's fine. But shoot five three-shot groups, and don't count groups with "called flyers"—shots that you *know* went astray because you let the cross hairs wobble.

For our purposes, after just a couple of range sessions we were done with the Model 700 ADL. Could we do a bit better? Probably, but now it would come down to work for a patient man— the "up a half-grain, down a half-grain, change primers" search for the perfect handload. This is Geoff Miller's meat and drink.

Working with Sierra Match Kings, benchrest primers, and the right charge of the right powder, I'm very certain he could get this rifle to shoot better than half-inch groups on a consistent basis. So what? We're still not going to win benchrest matches, and this is a *hunting rifle*. What we care about is hunting accuracy with hunting bullets, and we've achieved that. We could also have the barrel "cryo-ed," or perhaps Blackstarred. If this was *my* rifle that I wanted to hunt with for the rest of my life, I might consider either or both. On the other hand, this is a .30-06, with an inherently long barrel life due to its moderate velocity, and it's a used rifle that has required small investment to bring it to this level. In fact, the only added investment was a bit of ammo and a recoil pad. Why spend more? If it was my rifle, I would take the time to find a handload that it shot as well as that Remington Extended Range, this because I like to handload, and I'd like to use a bullet of *my* choosing. But for all intents and purposes, this rifle is now complete.

It could have worked out differently. We might have seen no improvement whatsoever from our slight modifications—or we might have seen the groups open. Then what? Well, you could try "cryo" and you could try Blackstar. You could add more upward pressure (which this rifle apparently didn't like), or go the other way and free—float. You could try pillar-bedding. Some of these solutions might yield significant returns. But the chances are that gains, if any, would be very incremental. At some point you simply have to accept that you have maximized the accuracy of which your rifle is capable. If it's sufficient to give you the confidence you need for your hunting, then you have a hunting rifle. Only you can determine the accuracy you need to provide that confidence. In a large-caliber dangerous-game rifle, a four-inch group at one hundred yards may be more than adequate. In a long-range deer rifle, 1-inch groups may not be good enough. That's up to you to decide, and you should be reasonable in your expectations. Not all hunting rifles will deliver 1-inch groups . . . but not all hunting rifles *need to*. Only you can decide whether you have a hunting rifle or several pounds of junk.

═══ CHAPTER FOURTEEN ═══

TO BRAKE OR NOT TO BRAKE

Although we macho hunters hate to admit it, recoil is a very serious problem for most of us . . . and fear of recoil is one of the primary reasons for poor shooting. Obviously, recoil is a natural phenomenon. All rifles recoil, and the more powerful the rifle the more recoil it has. This is part of Newton's Law about "every action having an equal and opposite reaction."

Bullet weight and velocity are the primary factors in producing recoil, but gun weight is also significant. The quickest way to reduce recoil is to add gun weight, pure and simple. The mathematical formula for figuring recoil is a most complex one, taking into account gun weight, weight of powder charge, projectile weight, and velocity. You need a darned good calculator or a lot of scratch paper to work it out—but you don't need to be a mathematician to feel the difference. A .30-06 that weighs 8½ pounds will yield about twenty foot-pounds of recoil; a .30-06 weighing 6½ pounds will yield almost thirty foot-pounds. This is actual recoil.

Now, this does not mean that a 6½-pound .30-06 is a hard kicker. But at some level, a very light rifle can be totally unmanageable. For instance, I had a 6½-pound .416 that was built as a sort of "swamp rifle." It was wonderful to carry, but simply horrible to shoot. I did the math on it, and with a 400-grain bullet at 2,400 fps it was belting me with nearly a hundred foot-pounds of recoil!

Mind you, all the mathematical formulas can give you is sheer foot-pounds of recoil. We don't necessarily care how much recoil a rifle develops. What we care about is whether or not it hurts— and that's felt recoil. You can't do a great deal about the raw force of recoil; the foot-pounds of rearward energy are what they are, based primarily on gun weight, bullet weight, and bullet velocity. However, there's a lot we can do about the way those foot-pounds are transferred into our bodies.

These days the muzzle brake seems to be the most common solution for licking kick. Muzzle brakes—and there are many designs—all function by redirecting gases, usually through holes or ports at or near the muzzle. Generally speaking, we think of a muzzle brake as being a device added onto the barrel forward of the rifled portion. Porting, on the other hand, may be done in the rifled portion of the barrel. There are a whole bunch of muzzle brakes, and there have been a number of porting systems (although Larry Kelly's Mag-Na-Port system is by far the most common).

Although it may be un-macho to admit it, recoil is not fun. If you need to shoot powerful rifles, you must learn to deal with it . . . but everybody has a different "recoil threshold," and only you can decide at what point your shooting is adversely affected.

Mag-Na-Porting vents gases upward and back, significantly reducing muzzle rise. This has two very positive effects. First, it enables you to remain on target and "call your shot" much more easily. Second, and probably much more important, since muzzle rise is greatly reduced, so is the rifle's tendency to kick upward into your tender cheek. Recoil is directed straight back, into the shoulder, so felt recoil is less. My good friend and frequent hunting partner, Joe Bishop, absolutely swears by Mag-Na-Porting for his hunting rifles—and this system has the added advantage of being more or less invisible.

Most muzzle brakes are threaded onto the end of the barrel. The arrangements of the holes vary tremendously, and each maker (naturally!) claims that his brake is the most effective. Muzzle brakes are very effective in reducing felt recoil, generally more effective than porting. I don't like their looks. At all. So if I had a very pretty rifle that kicked too much, I'd have it ported before I'd screw a corncob on the end of the muzzle. But that's personal preference.

Either way, I do feel that porting systems and muzzle brakes should be the last resort for reducing recoil, not the standard answer. Mind you, this is my opinion. Porting works, and in sheer recoil reduction muzzle brakes work better, so if you don't mind their looks and you want the recoil reduction they offer, be my guest . . . but please don't go hunting with me! My problem with muzzle brakes is that they are extremely noisy. Yes, I know, decibel-level tests don't always show this, but it isn't a matter of how much sound, but where it goes. Rifles are noisy. Redirection of the expanding gases redirects the noise. The shooter will notice a difference, but these things are really nasty on bystanders.

At this writing I've had two hunting situations where a muzzle-braked rifle was fired very close to my right ear. The first time was in Texas about ten years ago, when fellow writer Ross Seyfried fired a .416 Weatherby Magnum at a nilgai with the muzzle maybe twenty inches from my ear. The nilgai went down,

Recoil is greatly exaggerated if you shoot from the prone position, so muzzle brakes make sense on long-range rifles. This is the Browning Ballistic Optimizing Shooting System, an effective (and noisy) muzzle brake that also acts as an adjustable barrel weight for "tuning" a rifle to a given load.

but so did I. Just last year a whitetail hunter I was guiding had an accidental discharge with a muzzle-braked .300 Weatherby. This time the muzzle was much closer. Again I went down, hard. I cannot judge the specific hearing loss from those two incidents, but I know it was considerable. So was the pain and the irritating ringing in my ears that lasted for several days. Twice was enough; I don't want a third. So I don't ever again want to hunt with anyone who has a muzzle-braked rifle, and I hope I can avoid the necessity.

This is not to say that I'm altogether against muzzle brakes. They work, and if you want a fairly light rifle that is also very powerful, this may be your best option. If you hunt alone, or if you can coax your buddy into wearing hearing protection, then the noise probably doesn't matter, but if you go on a lot of guided hunts, then you may run into problems. I know of several very good African professional hunters who simply will not allow a muzzle brake in camp. I don't blame them; in addition to the PH himself, there are usually trackers and gunbearers close-by when a shot is taken, and it would be altogether too easy to break somebody's eardrum. Mag-Na-Porting is noisy, but since most of the sound is directed upward instead of sideways, I don't think this system is as obnoxious.

Sometimes a brake is the only option. I fought that ultralight .416 for quite a while before I gave in, but ultimately had little choice. I had a KDF muzzle brake put on it, and that tamed it right down to almost manageable. Similarly, I have a wonderfully accurate .300 Winchester Magnum from Match Grade Arms. The company uses benchrest technology but specializes in very light rifles. This particular rifle weighs in at about 6½ pounds with a 3-9X scope, and it regularly groups around ⅜-inch. It has a muzzle brake, which is the one thing I don't like about the rifle—but without the brake it would be an extremely unmanageable beast.

The Weatherby AccuMark in .30-.378 comes standard with a detachable muzzle brake and a thread protector; the idea is that you can practice with the brake on, then remove it for hunting. The only caution is that point of impact can change when you remove the brake.

There are innumerable arrangements of holes in muzzle brakes. The muzzle blast, and the effectiveness, varies somewhat with the arrangement of the holes, but all that I've seen work well—and are noisier than a plain barrel. This is the integral brake on a Christensen Arms "Carbon Cannon."

Depending on bullet weight and velocity, the recoil energy is around fifty foot-pounds, more than most .375 H&H rifles deliver. With the brake, it's a pussycat to shoot . . . but the muzzle blast is enough to take the paint off a barn door.

After my most recent "accident" with a muzzle brake I'm pretty much done with the darned things. If that's the only way to make a rifle shootable, I think I'd just as soon go to a lighter caliber, a heavier rifle, or both. However, this is a very personal decision. Muzzle brakes are extremely popular today because they work, and I have no issue with their use . . . provided you don't plan on using them around me!

Other than noise and unsightliness, there are no real drawbacks to a muzzle brake. They do not affect velocity in any way—provided you understand that your barrel length, insofar as velocity is concerned, ends where the rifling ends. Your muzzle brake will extend a couple of inches more, but it has nothing to do with velocity. The effect on accuracy is also neutral—sort of. In the way that all barrels are rules unto themselves, some barrels will shoot better after they've been "braked" and others will shoot worse—but there's no uniform effect. One thing to keep in mind, though, is that point of impact can change dramatically when the muzzle brake is attached or detached.

This makes sense; the muzzle brake is a weight at the end of the barrel, and it alters the way a barrel vibrates. This is neither negative nor positive; it just is. This is the principle that governs Browning's Ballistic Optimizing Shooting System (BOSS). You move the weight forward and back, altering the vibrations and essentially tailoring them to your load. If your muzzle brake is integral, you'll never know whether your rifle would shoot differently without it. But if you plan to practice with the muzzle brake and then remove it for hunting (which is a very good idea!), then you must remember to do your final sighting in without the brake. This can be a most painful experience if your rifle really needs a brake, but the difference in impact can be fairly dramatic. John Lazzeroni's rifles are generally equipped with detachable muzzle brakes, and he is the only maker I know who provides a test target showing groups with and without muzzle brake. A difference in point of impact of about 2 inches at 100 yards seems to be average. So if you don't have time to experiment, leave the damn thing on or off.

Though the muzzle brake is certainly one of the best ways to reduce felt recoil, it is not the only way. An extra pound of gun weight makes a huge difference, but stock design makes even more difference. The best way to reduce *felt* recoil is with a very straight stock that brings recoil straight back into the shoulder, coupled with a butt that is deep and wide to spread recoil out over as large an area as possible, plus a smooth, gentle comb that won't bruise the cheek. The A-Square "Coil-Chek" stock was designed by A-Square's Art Alphin to be the utmost in recoil attenuation. It is not the sleekest stock ever designed, or the lightest. OK, the truth is that the A-Square stock is ugly and heavy. But it *works*. A-Square rifles—without muzzle brakes—are the softest-recoiling rifles I have ever messed with. This is done strictly with gun weight and stock design.

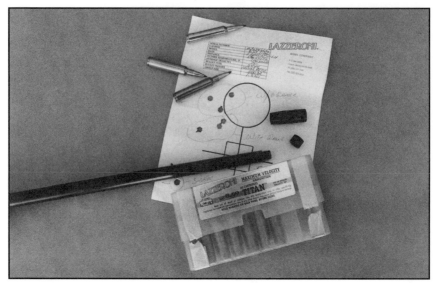

John Lazzeroni supplies a test target with his rifles that shows a group with and without the muzzle brake. A noticeable difference in point of impact can usually be seen.

Now, if you want a very trim stock, you can keep the recoil coming straight back, but the trimmer the butt the more the recoil will be concentrated in a smaller area. A good rubber recoil pad helps tremendously, and one made from the newer shock-absorbing polymers (like Pachmayr's Decelerator and the Sorb-A-Coil pad) helps even more than rubber. I'm not recoil-sensitive, so the addition of a good rubber pad onto the wooden-stocked Model 700 ADL is the only alteration I needed for recoil attenuation in a .30-06. This rifle came from the factory with a hard buttplate, which not only did nothing for recoil but also slipped badly every time I cheeked the rifle. A good rubber pad helped in both areas, and was all that was required *for my tastes*. The synthetic-stocked Model 700 came from the factory with a standard one-inch rifle pad, and needed nothing additional—as far as I'm concerned.

All of us have different "recoil thresholds," so I'm certainly not implying that a very standard .30-06 might not have too much recoil for somebody—perhaps for a whole bunch of somebodies! But these work fine for me. This situation is greatly aided by the fact that I'm of very average build, and standard factory stock dimensions fit me quite well. Both of these rifles have relatively straight stocks that were designed in anticipation of use with a scope, so both come up nicely with the eye centered on the scope and the cheek welded to the stock, which also helps. The wooden-stocked ADL has a Monte Carlo comb, meaning that this rifle has a bit more drop at heel, while the fiberglass-stocked rifle has a straight "classic-style" comb. Although the difference is subtle, I believe that the wooden-stocked rifle, despite being slightly heavier, delivers more felt recoil than the synthetic-stocked gun. However, both of these rifles are perfectly comfortable to shoot.

What if they weren't? The options are not endless, but there are a few things you can do. First (and simplest, and cheapest) is a better recoil pad. There really is a big difference between no pad, a rubber pad, and a modern pad like a Decelerator. If the rifle is still beating you up and you're sure it isn't a stock-fit problem, you really have just two ways to go. You can keep the

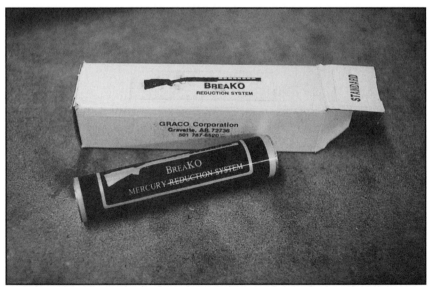

An alternative to a muzzle brake is the mercury piston. This is the BreaKO, an extremely effective device. Depending on the recoil, from one to three can be used. However, there's a trade-off: Each Break-O weighs 14 ounces!

rifle at its present weight and use redirected gases to attenuate recoil—meaning either have the gun ported or have a muzzle brake installed. Or you can add gun weight. Obviously neither choice is perfect.

As we've seen, when you redirect the gases, you make the rifle more noisier—if not for you, then for your hunting buddies. Also, though neither porting nor any muzzle brake I'm aware of has any real impact on accuracy, keep in mind that *anything* you do to a rifle barrel is likely to *change* accuracy. It could make it better or it could make it worse. Heck, it might even remain the same. If you have a rifle of average accuracy it probably doesn't matter—but if you happen to have a rifle that shoots exceptionally well, then you should think long and hard before you do *anything* to its barrel.

Adding gun weight also isn't a perfect solution. Keeping in mind that we're talking about hunting rifles, whatever weight you add will have to be carried wherever the rifle is carried! But don't underestimate the difference an extra pound can make toward getting recoil down to a manageable level.

I'm not particularly recoil-sensitive, as mentioned, so the .30-06 rifles we're working with make a poor example. But I can give you good examples of rifles that I've had to tame down—and, depending on the rifle's purpose, I've followed both of these paths in doing so. I mentioned that ultralight .416 earlier. It had a Parkerized finish and a classic-styled synthetic stock, and it handled like a dream. Unfortunately the barrel was all hole. It just kicked like hell, and it ate scope mounts like they were popcorn. I didn't want to add gun weight. So I added the KDF muzzle brake. The result was predictable: The rifle got real noisy. But finally I could shoot it without gritting my teeth and shutting my eyes.

Another rifle I once had was a bolt-action chambered to .458 Lott, a wildcat firing a 500-grain bullet at about 2,350 fps. It was stocked in beautiful walnut, and had a very stiff barrel. However,

Stock style makes a huge difference in felt recoil, but so does a good recoil pad. The only modification made to our much-used Model 700 ADL was the addition of a good, thick recoil pad—and even at .30-06 recoil levels the difference was dramatic.

it was set up for iron sights and had no scope or mount, so all there was to give it weight was action, barrel, and a fairly trim classic-styled stock. Even with relatively fancy (and thus heavy) wood and a stiff barrel, it weighed under nine pounds. This is too light for a rifle of this power level, and the recoil was ferocious. Jack Lott himself took the rifle and inletted some nooks and crannies in both the fore-end and butt, eventually pouring in about a pound and a half of molten lead to bring the weight up to ten pounds. The difference was dramatic.

Again, the drawback to weight is that you have to carry it. Perhaps of equal significance is that you can't just willy-nilly add weight without impacting gun balance and heft. On that .458 we added weight very carefully, in both butt and fore-end, so that the balance was maintained. You always must keep this factor in mind when adding weight, but there is a much more effective way to add weight than just by pouring in molten lead. Trapshooters have been using mercury-piston recoil reducers for years, but riflemen have apparently just recently discovered them.

The mercury piston doesn't actually reduce the foot-pounds of recoil, except by the amount that its weight naturally reduces recoil. However, the effect is to spread the recoil impulse out over a few more milliseconds—and it's dramatic. The one that I'm most familiar with is the Break-O, sold by Brownell's. A cylinder about the size of two end-to-end 12-gauge shells, it weighs fully 14 ounces. My buddy Geoff Miller absolutely swears by these gadgets. He puts two in his .470 and .500 Nitro Express double rifles, and the effect is dramatic. Art Alphin also recommends them, especially for his behemoth .577 Tyrannosaur rifles, and Kreighoff offers them as a factory option in its double rifles as well.

I have just one in the butt of my Rogue River 8mm Remington Magnum, and I can definitely feel the difference. Fourteen ounces—nearly a pound—is quite a bit extra to carry up a sheep mountain. Personally, I would slip a Break-O in the butt and carry the extra weight long before I'd put a muzzle brake on a rifle—especially if we're talking about fairly standard calibers (and normal recoil), where just one 14-ounce device will achieve the desired results. But that's a personal decision, and the rules are pretty simple: First, if the recoil is uncomfortable, you should do something about it. Second, if you have to keep the gun light, then porting or muzzle braking is almost certainly your best option. Third, any weight you add, whether a Break-O or simple ballast, becomes a permanent part of the rifle that must not only be carried but also will alter the balance for better or worse. It's up to you to decide what steps you should take—but don't put up with more recoil than you can handle. Poor shooting is the only possible result, and none of us can afford that!

═══ CHAPTER FIFTEEN ═══

SELECTING FACTORY LOADS

Steve Hornady of Hornady Bullets is one of my oldest and dearest friends in the industry. At the Shooting, Hunting, and Outdoor Trade (SHOT) Show just this year we were talking about the business, and he lamented that "not enough people are handloading any more." I hadn't thought about this, but as a bulletmaker Steve thinks about it every day. The reality is that factory ammo has gotten so good and so diverse that the justification to handload isn't nearly as strong as it was when I started shooting.

I still handload—"for fun and profit," as it were, since I still enjoy reloading *and* I still believe there's plenty of justification for rolling your own. We'll talk about handloading in the next chapter, and I'll tell you why I still go to the trouble. Then you can make up your own mind. If you decide handloading isn't worth the trouble—or the significant downstroke in equipment—I will surely understand. But let's talk about factory ammo.

One aspect that used to make a very strong argument for handloading is greater diversity in bullet selection. This doesn't hold near as much water today. Factory ammo will never offer as wide a selection of bullets as is available to the handloader, but the gap grows ever more narrow. For many years the major manufacturers concentrated on marketing the mystique of their own brand names and trademarked bullets. Winchester had

Silvertip and Power Point; Remington had Core-Lokt and Bronze Point; Federal had Hi-Shok. Mixed in, but *quietly,* were bullets sourced from Hornady, Sierra, and others. Federal changed the rules when it started naming names, offering Federal Premium loads with Sierra Boattails and Nosler Partitions.

That was a long time ago. Now you can get darn near any bullet—or bullet properties—that you want in factory ammo. You can get Nosler Partitions, Trophy Bonded Bearclaws, Swift A-Frames, Nosler Ballistic Tips, Barnes X Bullets, Sierra Boattails, and Hornady Interlocks in a wide variety of factory loads. And you'll find a whole new (and often bewildering) array of "designer bullets" under the manufacturers' own brand names: Winchester Fail Safe and Ballistic Silvertip; Remington Extended Range.

Factory ammo has not only gotten incredibly varied but also so consistent—so *good*—that it is very hard to beat in the accuracy department on a load-for-load basis. However, there are some things you should keep in mind when you begin the search for the perfect factory load. First off, although the selection can be totally bewildering, it is not truly as diverse as it looks. Factory loads are still "vanilla ice cream," although they may have fudge sauce and even sprinkles on top. What I mean by this is that, though you may be able to find darn near any bullet you want in a factory load, at least in the most common cartridges, *you will probably find that bullet featured in just one load from one manufacturer.*

As we've already seen, rifles aren't just finicky—they can be downright perverse. You may want to shoot a Winchester Fail Safe, or a Nosler Partition, or a Core-Lokt, or any other bullet you care to name in your rifle. If you don't care about optimizing accuracy, you can do that. But if you want your rifle to shoot reasonably close to its potential, here's the problem: There is absolutely no guarantee that your rifle will perform at its best with the one factory load that features the bullet of your dreams.

So here are some basic rules for choosing and using factory loads. First, if you don't intend to handload, choose a cartridge for which a wide selection of factory loads is available. Second,

Steve Hornady in his ammunition manufacturing facility in Grand Island, Nebraska. Factory ammunition has gotten so good that the justification to handload is not nearly so strong as it used to be.

choose your loads by desired performance characteristics, not by specific brand name. Third, experiment with as wide a variety of factory loads as possible *that offer these characteristics* before making your choice. Let's examine these rules in greater detail.

As we've discussed in previous chapters, a lot of our very popular hunting cartridges are actually quite similar in performance on game . . . especially if you can compare like bullets. This is not always possible in factory ammo. There are some very good cartridges out there that have never achieved widespread popularity . . . and you won't find a wide selection of factory loads, let alone upgraded ammo featuring the premium and "super premium" bullets. For instance, my buddy Geoff Miller will argue all day that his old .300 H&H—he calls it the "Death Ray"—is the equal of any .300 Winchester Magnum. He's right—with his handloads. But .300 H&H factory loads are so few today that this grand old cartridge is a very foolish choice for shooters who don't handload.

One of the tricky things about factory ammo is that a given load is just that—a given load. Your rifle may not shoot the bullet you would most like to use in that given factory load, so for best results you need to be somewhat flexible. This Browning hated Fail Safe, but shot well with other Winchester factory loads.

Among my own favorites, I suggest that both the 6.5x55 Swede and the 7x57 Mauser are very poor choices for shooters who don't handload. Most factory loads for both cartridges are loaded to very mild pressures and low velocities because of potential use in very old military Mausers. With good handloads in sound rifles, both cartridges are wonderfully efficient and effective—but shooters who stick with factory loads are losing a lot of the potential of both cartridges. And although it was never a military cartridge, much the same can be said of the good old .257 Roberts.

Factory-load selection is getting better for the .25-06 and .280 Remington, and even for the .35 Whelen, but the variety is not overly generous. Among the lineup of Weatherby Magnums, only the .300 offers a reasonably wide selection—but it will never compare with the .300 Winchester Magnum. The 7mm-08 is a wonderful cartridge, and so are the 6mm

Remington and the new .260 Remington, but there are few loads for either. In fact, if you are really serious about (1) sticking with factory ammo and (2) maximizing your rifle's performance, I suggest that your list of desirable cartridges be very short: In varmint cartridges, .223 and .22-250 Remington; in "dual-purpose" varmint/small big-game rounds, .243 Winchester; in big-game cartridges, .270 Winchester, 7mm Remington Magnum, .30-30 Winchester, .308 Winchester, .30-06 Springfield, .300 Winchester Magnum, .300 Weatherby Magnum, .338 Winchester Magnum, .375 H&H Magnum. That's just twelve cartridges out of the incredibly wide spectrum of available choices. Understand that I am not suggesting that these are the "best" hunting cartridges in any context, although all are very good. They are simply the most popular, which means everybody loads for them, and the permutations of bullets and brands are darn near endless. And while there are many other great hunting cartridges, these do cover just about all hunting worldwide. The only thing missing is a large-caliber cartridge, but here all you should care about is ammo that's available with a good softpoint and a good solid; it isn't essential to maximize the accuracy of a .416, .458, or .470.

OK, so let's say you've chosen a cartridge that is available in a wide variety of factory loads. You haven't actually made your job easier. For instance, if you have an 8mm Remington Magnum, you're going to go to the gunshop and hope against hope that you can find a box of Remington factory ammo—and you'll be thankful if there's a dusty old box somewhere on the shelf.

But let's assume that you don't have a rifle chambered to a cartridge that requires searching for leftover boxes of ammo of unknown vintage—and hoarding them when you find them. Instead, your rifle is chambered to a cartridge that is a popular commodity. All the ammunition manufacturers load for it, and all the outlets carry it. If, as a for-instance, your rifle happened to be chambered to .30-06, I'm quite sure you could find at least fifty different factory loads without searching all that hard. If you included smaller and specialty manufacturers, I'm certain you could double that.

This can be confusing. And I suspect it's even more confusing for shooters who stick with factory loads than it is for veteran handloaders. The latter group has studied load data, played with chronographs, and worked up loads for a variety of bullets, and is less likely (I think) to walk into a sporting goods store and say, "Gimme a box of '06 shells." The former group, those who exclusively use factory ammo, *can* achieve results on a par with even the most astute handloaders—but they need to be systematic in their approach, and they have to go far beyond "Gimme a box of '06 shells."

All important is for you to know what you want. This is the first step in my Rule Two, categorizing factory loads by performance characteristics. This is not quite as difficult as it sounds. For instance, if you want a bunch of ammo to go plinking at the dump—without undue concern about group size and *no* worries about bullet performance—then you're going to shop for the cheapest ammo available. If your rifle is a .308 or .30-06 you may be able to latch onto some military ball ammo. In other cartridges you'll have to shop around . . . but you won't be buying premium loads!

If you want raw accuracy, again without regard to bullet performance, then you have a tough job ahead of you. Whether the total number is 10, 50, or 100, each factory load for a given cartridge represents *one* specific blend of powder, primer, and bullet. They are designed to perform consistently and reliably, and will shoot "OK" in most rifles. Some will shoot very well in a given rifle and some will not . . . and it is impossible to predict which will be the winners and which the losers.

Sure, there are trends. Hornady ammunition, though more limited in both variety and availability than ammo from the three "majors" (Federal, Remington, Winchester), generally shoots extremely well. The "upgraded" ammo generally shoots well:

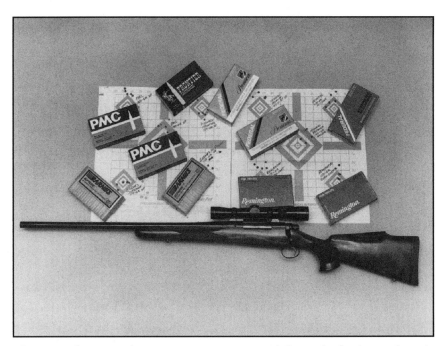

If you're really serious about optimizing accuracy with factory loads, the search can be exhaustive (and expensive!). These groups range from just over an inch to nearly three inches. Any given rifle will shoot differently with different loads, but this is a very normal range for an accurate bolt-action.

Federal Premium, Winchester Supreme, Remington Extended Range. Speer's Nitrex, loaded with tough Grand Slam bullets, generally shoots very well. None of this guarantees the best results in *your* rifle.

Of all the loads I've tried in it, my own .30-06 from the Remington Custom Shop groups best with standard 165-grain Remington Core-Lokt loads. Another .30-06 we were testing some time back exasperated us completely until we tried "red box" Federal with 150-grain Hi-Shok bullets. That rifle liked *that* load—and not much else! A Dakota .270 I was testing really liked Winchester's 150-grain Power Point load . . . but my own Dakota .270, a visually identical rifle, much prefers Remington Extended Range. If group size is your goal, leave no stone unturned; there's no predicting exactly which factory load will produce the best results in a given rifle.

Fortunately most of us have a more specific goal in mind than sheer accuracy, which should help narrow the search pattern significantly. Since we're talking about hunting rifles, chances are you have at least a class of game in mind—if not a specific upcoming hunt—so you probably want to start with at least a general bullet weight range.

For most hunting purposes this will be the bullet weights that are medium for caliber. The light bullets (80 grains and below in 6mm; 100 grains in .270; 120 grains and below in 7mm; 130 grains and below in .30) are generally fast-expanding varmint bullets. The heaviest bullets in a given caliber are often not loaded in factory ammo, but if they are—like the 220-grain .30-caliber— you can assume that these are very special-purpose loads for close-range hunting of the very largest game. So, by discounting the lightest and heaviest loads, you're left with a medium or medium-to-heavy weight range in a given caliber. In .243, this should be 95 to 105 grains; in .270, it's 130 to 150 grains; in 7mm, it's 140 to 175 grains; in .30, it's 150 to 200 grains. You can easily trim the list further by considering the game you plan to hunt. If you're after small-bodied deer or pronghorns, the lighter weights within these ranges are probably best suited. If you're after elk or bear, the heavier weights are obviously best. For general purposes, stick to the middle of the road.

At some point you probably want to consider bullet shape. These days most of us automatically choose an aerodynamic sharp-pointed bullet if such is available. For all-round use this is clearly the best decision—but not always. A good old round-nose bullet transfers energy more quickly and decisively than a sharp-pointed bullet, so if you know you're not going to shoot very far you might consider a round-nose. Examples such as black bear from a baited stand, timber elk hunting, or even close-cover hunting for big whitetails come to mind. Despite its very modest ballistics, the old .30-30 with its flat-nose bullets hits very hard, and part of the reason is the energy transfer caused by the blunt nose. Round-nose bullets also make a difference, and there are factory loads available in most popular calibers and bullet weights. Don't rule them out—but keep in mind that blunt-nose bullets shed velocity *much* faster than spitzers, so avoid them like the plague for open-country use.

Don't, on the other hand, get all wrapped up about boattail bullets. The boattail does shoot a bit flatter than a flat-based bullet, but it was actually designed for long-range use in machine guns, and its major benefit is reducing turbulence when the bullet drops below the sound barrier. In modern calibers this happens *far* beyond hunting ranges. At the ranges at which game is shot—even out past 400 yards—the difference between a spitzer boattail and a spitzer flat-base is almost never more than a couple of inches. The primary reason to shoot a boattail rather than a flat-based bullet is *because it shoots better in your rifle*—but don't automatically assume this will be so.

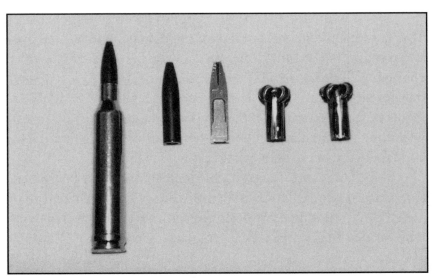

This is the famed Winchester Fail Safe bullet, shown sectioned and with bullet recovered at 200 and 300 yards. This is one of several super-tough "super-premium" bullets—but your rifle may not shoot this particular bullet in its particular factory load. More importantly, you may not need this level of toughness in a bullet.

This Beretta Mato in .270 was extremely consistent, producing nearly identical groups with a variety of factory loads. If you happen to have a rifle this non-finicky with factory ammo, cherish it!

Along with bullet shape you need to consider bullet design. This is probably the most complex subject and, with all the hype surrounding new bullet designs, certainly one of the most confusing. Let's forget all the hype and begin with a statement that might startle you: There are no "bad bullets" available in factory loads. Virtually all factory-loaded bullets will do exactly what they're supposed to do. The hard part is cutting through the hype to figure out exactly what that is.

Some bullets are designed to expand more quickly than others; some are designed for very controlled expansion and deep penetration; still others are designed for maximum aerodynamics, with terminal performance a secondary consideration. The size of game makes a difference; you need a "tougher" bullet for elk than you do for pronghorn—but your cartridge also makes a difference. Good bullet performance is almost a given at .308 Winchester and/or .30-06 velocities—but load the same bullet in a .300 Winchester or Weatherby Magnum and expansion may be much more rapid. *Now* are you confused?

With every major manufacturer offering "name" bullets in higher-priced ammo lines, it's easy to ignore the "brand name" bullets that my generation grew up with. Let's start with them. In the Remington line, the Core-Lokt was (and is) the standard bullet for controlled expansion. The Bronze Point, still loaded in a few cartridges, was designed for much more rapid expansion. The Core-Lokt is a very good bullet, especially at "standard" velocities. Similarly, Federal's Hi-Shok is a very good bullet, especially at non-magnum velocities. And so is Winchester's Power Point. I still consider the Core-Lokt, Hi-Shok, and Power Point as the "baseline" for ideal bullet performance on *normal-size game* in *standard calibers* at *normal ranges*. If you're after large or tough game (read "bigger and tougher than deer"), you're shooting fast magnum cartridges, or you want top performance at long range (and especially if you combine more than one of these factors), you may want to consider trying some of today's "factory super-loads." But try to get a handle on exactly what it is you're trying to accomplish.

Again, I tend to sort ammunition into loads designed for penetration and performance on very large game, and loads that are likely to be more accurate and offer good expansion even at long range. While accuracy is always wonderful, keep in mind that you need less accuracy on moose and elk than you do on pronghorn and sheep—but you need more controlled bullet expansion!

When I think about loads designed for deep penetration on large, tough game—especially from fast-magnum cartridges—I'm thinking about: Barnes X Bullets (El Dorado and Weatherby ammunition); Speer Grand Slam (Speer Nitrex); Swift A-Frame Bullets (Remington Safari); Trophy Bonded Bearclaw (Federal Premium) and Nosler Partition (Federal Premium and Weatherby); and Winchester Fail Safe (Winchester Supreme). When I think about loads most likely to deliver long-range accuracy and bullet expansion at long range, I'm thinking about Hornady Interlock (Hornady and Weatherby); Nosler Ballistic Tip (Federal Premium and Remington); Ballistic Silvertip (Winchester Supreme); Sierra Boattail (Federal Premium); and Remington Extended Range. In other words, if I was specifically looking for a load for moose, bear, or general-purpose African plains game, I'd look to the first group. If I was after pronghorn, sheep, or open-country deer, I'd look to the second group. And if I just wanted a good general-purpose load, I'd go for a fairly heavy-for-caliber spitzer . . . and in my search I would *not* overlook the good old "vanilla ice cream" loads featuring such bullets as Federal Hi-Shok, Remington Core-Lokt, and Winchester Power Point.

The chronograph is usually thought of as a handloader's tool, but chronographs have gotten so simple and inexpensive that they're also excellent for factory ammo shooters who care about performance. Only a chronograph can tell you what a given load is actually doing in your rifle—and the variance between reality and published figures can be surprising.

Which brings us to Boddington's Third Rule in selecting factory ammo: Now that you know what you want, you need to try as many loads as possible that offer the characteristics you have in mind. It would be nice if you could study the catalogs and ballistics charts and decide on the perfect load in a vacuum. Perhaps you can, in terms of the bullet performance you want— but your rifle may shoot that load horribly. So you need to experiment with a *class* of loads in the near-certainty that some will shoot better than others in your rifle. A good example is the increased-velocity loads now offered by both Hornady (Light Magnum and Heavy Magnum) and Federal (High Energy) in some popular calibers. These loads are faster than "standard" factory loads by a very considerable margin. Both Federal's and Hornady's "hopped-up" 180-grain .30-06 load is rated at 2,880 fps, an increase of 180 fps over the "standard" 2,700-fps load. Good heavens, why would you consider shooting anything else? Unfortunately, no given factory load will group equally well (or even acceptably well!) in all rifles.

Our synthetic-stocked Model 700 .30-06 provided a very good example of this perversity. It simply didn't like the Federal High-Energy loads, but it grouped exceptionally well with Remington's Extended Range 178-grain load. In fact, it grouped *so* well that this load, in this rifle, was an instant "look no farther" choice for open-country work. Given that the caliber is a .30-06, delivering moderate velocity that yields consistent bullet performance, and given also that the 178-grain bullet is fairly heavy for this caliber, this particular load would do just fine for almost anything a .30-06 is suitable for. However, if a tougher bullet was desired for large game, the same round of tests indicated that Speer Nitrex with 180-grain Grand Slam bullets shot very well, as did Federal Premium with 180-grain Nosler. Nope, not quite as good as the sub-half-inch groups that Extended Range stuff delivered, but plenty good for most hunting purposes.

Does this mean that you need to buy—and try—a half-dozen boxes of factory ammo before making a choice? That depends on how picky you are. You can try just one, and if the groups are acceptable, you're home free. If your "first choice" doesn't work, you can go on down the list one at a time. In any case, I do not recommend that you go out to the range with ten boxes of factory ammo all at once. Especially in heavy-recoiling, big-game calibers, nobody is capable of shooting all that many good groups in a given day. Instead, take your time and try just one or two loads in a given session. Record (or keep) your groups, making notes regarding wind conditions and even whether you were shooting particularly well or badly on that day. Make sure you let your barrel cool properly between groups, and make sure you clean your rifle periodically.

Yes, this is all very time-consuming. If you get really lucky, you may strike paydirt on the first go—but you should still try a couple of other loads. Heck, it might do even better, or you might have one of those rare treasures that groups pretty well no matter what you feed it! Ultimately there will be some waste. Chances are you'll run into at least one factory load that is absolutely useless in your rifle—and you'll know it before the typical box of twenty rounds is half done. I'm not much on sending unnecessary bullets down rifle barrels, so my garage is full of half-empty boxes of ammo. Mark the boxes—or mark the bases with color-coded lacquer—and use them for fouling shots, *very* casual practice, or save them for a buddy who has a rifle in that caliber.

Remember, just because a given load doesn't group well in your rifle doesn't mean that it won't group well in every other rifle of that caliber in the whole world! That's the frustrating part of choosing factory loads; the load you most want to use may be the most hopeless in your rifle. On the other hand, if you keep an open mind, the choice today is so broad that, at least in popular calibers, there will almost certainly be several factory loads well suited to your purpose. The trick is to be persistent enough to find the best possible combination of accuracy and bullet performance.

══ CHAPTER SIXTEEN ══

HANDLOADING FOR HUNTING

In the previous chapter I admitted that the justification for handloading is no longer as strong as it once was. Like everything else, prices of reloading equipment have gone up considerably, as have components. Cartridge by cartridge, you still save a lot of money by handloading, and the more you shoot the more you save. However, I suspect that it takes a whole lot longer to amortize the startup costs today than it did when I was a kid. Of course, my own equipment has long since paid for itself . . . many times over. I've replaced a few pieces of equipment over the years, but one of my presses and several sets of dies are now more than thirty years old!

I will freely admit that in some cases I handload purely to save money. Factory ammunition for my .416 Rigby costs about five bucks a pop; ammo for the big doubles is even more expensive. I believe my handloads are just as reliable, and depending on which bullets I use, I can cut the cost down to as low as two dollars a round. Those large calibers are exceptions: With paid-for equipment and lots of brass for most calibers, I *always* save money handloading—but this is not a primary motivation.

Partly I do it because I enjoy the activity. My mind is always racing a hundred miles an hour, with multiple deadlines to meet, photos to sort, Marine Corps business to tend to, and God knows what else. Handloading is one of few activities I engage in that allows me to escape from day-to-day hassles and concentrate strictly on the moment. This, by the way, is how it has to be. You can't handload safely while watching a football game or while your mind is wandering elsewhere. You simply must *concentrate* on what you're doing. If you do this, plus develop a systematic approach and keep your work area scrupulously clear of all components except those for the load you're working on, then you can't make much of a mistake. Handloading is not rocket science. It is more aptly described as mindless repetition, which is why I enjoy it; I find it a restful and productive activity.

I also believe that I can load better ammo than I can buy. And let me qualify that statement very carefully. I believe my handloads are just as reliable as factory loads—but I sure can't say they're better in that department. Factory loads are so incredibly reliable today that misfires, hangfires, and faulty cartridges are just darn near unheard of. Or, better put, they are so rare that when they occur it's cause for remarking. I believe my handloads are perhaps slightly more consistent than most factory loads, and certainly as accurate—this because I load all of my hunting ammo the old-fashioned way, by weighing each and every charge.

However, factory ammo is so good and so consistent today that I make no claim that I can *always* beat it. Here are some examples of how good factory ammo *can be* today. Geoff Miller has a Remington 40XB in .243. The 40XB is a kind of "super Model 700" action; it's a single-shot version, so it's very stiff, and they are made to match specifications. This rifle is a known "quarter-inch" rifle, meaning that it will produce quarter-inch and smaller groups on a regular basis with loads that it likes. Geoff was curious about the new Winchester Supreme .243 load with the light-for-caliber 55-grain Ballistic Silvertip bullet. We both agreed that, being that light, it couldn't possibly group well . . . but what the heck?

Oh, my Lord! The entire box grouped well under a half-inch, with the average running about a third of an inch—and a couple under a quarter of an inch. Geoff does indeed know a few handload recipes for this rifle that will beat that average. But how good is good enough? He's not using the rifle for benchrest competition, but for shooting ground squirrels. Geoff immediately ordered a case of this ammunition, swearing that he'll never handload for this rifle again.

The synthetic-stocked Remington Model 700 that I've been playing with for this book is another good example. We tried several factory loads with reasonable results. One, the 178-grain Remington Extended Range load, groups well under a half-inch. I can *perhaps* equal this with some good handloads. *Maybe* I can better it . . . but why try? With factory loads this rifle delivers all the accuracy I could possibly want out of a .30-06. Attempting to make measurable improvement is not only pointless, but could also prove very frustrating.

Handloading is not a complex process. The keys to success are keeping the workbench free of everything except what you're doing at the moment—and keeping your mind free of clutter as well. If you concentrate on what you're doing it's difficult to make a mistake.

On the other hand, not all rifles will shoot their best with a store-bought "vanilla ice cream" load—at least not without going through an exhaustive and expensive array of loads. The real advantage to handloading is not cost savings or raw accuracy or reliability, but rather the opportunity to *tailor a load to an individual rifle*. With factory ammunition, you simply must find a load that your rifle likes, and if you search hard enough (and there are enough choices available in your caliber), you can probably find one. With handloads, you can tailor a load to your rifle, and if you do it right the results can be quite spectacular.

Mind you, our discussion is relative to big-game rifles and hunting ammunition; we're not trying to win benchrest matches, or shoot prairie dogs at four hundred yards. Good enough is good enough, and today factory ammo is so good and will fail to satisfy so few rifles that you can almost always find a satisfactory factory load. On the other hand, there is value in knowing how well your rifle really will shoot, plus there is no substitute for

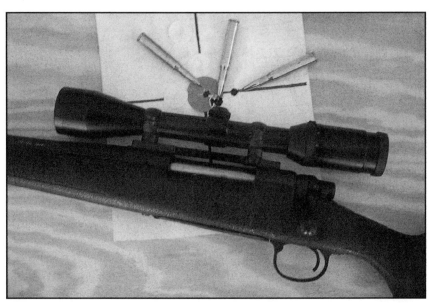

This is my Kenny Jarrett .30-06. It shoots pretty well with factory loads, but with RL-15 powder, Federal Match primers, and Nosler Ballistic Tips, it's fabulous.

the confidence factor that comes from wonderfully tight groups. Hunting accuracy is possible with factory ammo, good handloads, and even fairly sloppy handloads. *Real* accuracy is a game for good handloads, period.

Though I am very impressed with the accuracy we are getting from both of our "project" Model 700s, neither is the most accurate .30-06 I own. That honor goes to a .30-06 that Kenny Jarrett built for me, of course on a Remington Model 700 left-hand action. This is not one of Jarrett's "Beanfield Rifles" but a standard-weight sporter with a synthetic stock and a fairly stiff barrel. I've tried a number of factory loads, and it's no problem finding a good hunting load that groups well under an inch. Best so far is Speer Nitrex with 180-grain Grand Slams, certainly a useful all-round hunting load. However, of several handload recipes I've tried, the most accurate so far is the load Kenny Jarrett gave me with the rifle: Winchester cases, 150-grain Nosler Ballistic Tip bullet, 53.5 grains of Hercules RL-15, and a Federal 210 Match primer. This load produces groups averaging .431-inch, which will not win benchrest contests but is very good for a .30-06. Wonderful cartridge though it is, the old '06 almost never develops match-quality accuracy.

My David Miller 7mm Remington Magnum is another good example of a rifle that responds well to good handloads. Again, this is a very fine rifle and not overly finicky. It will shoot groups of around an inch with many good factory loads. It particularly likes Hornady factory ammo with the 154-grain Spire Point bullet, and will produce groups very close to a half-inch. I suppose I don't need better than that, but with good handloads this rifle really talks. For years my favorite load was a maximum charge of Hodgdon H870 with Nosler's 162-grain Solid Base bullet. Regrettably, the company discontinued this fine bullet. I switched to 165-grain Sierra Boattails and, for heavier game, 160-grain Nosler Partitions. This remains my most accurate 7mm Remington Magnum load, and has proven so in several rifles. As you might expect, it will shoot both of these bullets into the same group, but the Nosler Partitions tend to group around a half-inch while the Sierras will beat that by quite a bit. H870 is a powder that burns fairly dirty, so in recent years I've been using a lot of Hercules RL22, generally 65 grains for a 160-grain bullet. Accuracy is not quite as good, but the barrel fouls much more slowly.

You will recall that both the 7mm Remington Magnum and the .30-06 were on my list of cartridges recommended for people who don't handload. I can load somewhat more accurate ammo than I can buy for the rifles mentioned above, but there are plenty of factory loads that are good enough for any and all hunting purposes. On the other hand, the most accurate rifle I own, and probably ever will own, is the long-barreled 8mm Remington Magnum Geoff Miller built for me. This rifle was intended for use with handloads, period. Historically there have been only three factory loads for the 8mm Remington Magnum—not nearly enough of a selection to ensure near-optimum results. The original offerings were a 220-grain Core-Lokt and a 185-grain Pointed Soft Point. The former load, a pretty good one, was discontinued, leaving only the light-for-caliber and (to my mind) useless 185-grain load. Last year Remington introduced a new 200-grain load, which has some promise, but we designed our 8mm around handloads with heavy bullets.

There aren't many, but there are enough. For accuracy and long-range performance, there's a 220-grain Sierra Boattail. For heavier game, there are two more 220-grain bullets: Barnes X and Swift A-Frame. Hornady also has a 220-grain interlock bullet. Geoff Miller, one of the more astute accuracy freaks I know, worked up the loads for this rifle. Using long-grain Hodgdon 4831 powder, Federal 215 Match primers, new brass, and 220-grain Sierra Boattails, I fired the best group of my life with this rifle, .052-inch (one-twentieth of an inch), in front of witnesses. Needless to say, it won't group like that every day, and it won't fire the Swift or X Bullets into that kind of a group. But with slightly adjusted powder charges it will shoot all three bullets into

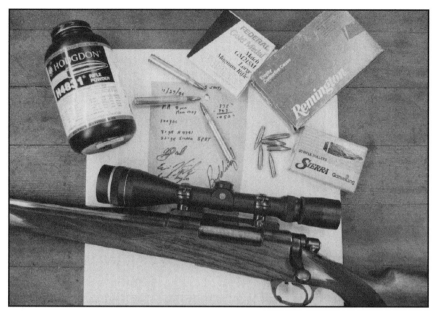

This is the best group I've ever shot, measuring a tidy .052-inch. The Rogue River 8mm Remington Magnum rifle is well built, but the real secrets are a Pac-Nor match-grade barrel and handloads that are carefully assembled and mated to the rifle.

the same sub-half-inch group, which makes this 8mm a very effective hunting rifle from point-blank to 600 yards, and for game from pronghorn to grizzly bear. It's still a relatively new rifle, but I've used it on Coues whitetails and elk, on Asian sheep and gazelles, and on African antelope from impala to eland. The point is, of course, that without handloads this rifle would not even exist!

It is not my purpose here to publish a "how to" manual for handloading. Neither the processes nor the tools are complicated. You do not need automated machines, and for hunting ammo I don't even recommend them. I still load all of my ammunition on a single-stage press, and this is plenty fast enough for my purposes. For hunting ammunition, consistency and reliability are far more important than volume. That said, every single reloading tool on the market, from the simplest hand tool to the most automated progressive machine, is capable of producing consistent, reliable, and accurate ammunition. The operator is of critical importance, and so is proper operation. Regardless of what system or setup you use, *read the directions*—not only for initial setup but each time you change something.

Come to think of it, the best handloaders probably aren't mechanical engineers but rather good readers. One of the most significant investments you must make is in a selection of good reloading manuals. I have manuals from Nosler, Speer, Sierra, Hornady, Barnes, A-Square, Lyman, Hodgdon, and more . . . and I use them all. In addition to load recipes, each one contains good "how to" sections that will help beginners get started, and can also help veterans solve problems that may occur.

These manuals, of course, are your primary source of information when selecting components for loading a given cartridge. You will probably find that they don't altogether agree; "maximum" loads may differ by several grains from one loading manual to another. This is because that load was "maximum" *in that company's test barrel*, nothing more and nothing less. I recommend that any powder charge listed as "maximum" in *any* manual be approached with caution; your rifle may not be able to handle quite as much as theirs, or it may take a grain or two more. The other thing to keep in mind, and a factor that many reloaders tend to ignore (sometimes with catastrophic results), is that published data only applies to the *exact* blend of components listed. You cannot take a given charge of, say, IMR 4350 powder listed in the Nosler manual for its 180-grain Partition in a .30-06 and expect the same pressures if you use Barnes, Hornady, or Speer bullets. For that matter, you cannot expect the same pressures if you change the brand of cases or primers, or if you change the seating depth or overall length. OK, let's get real: Since your action, chamber, and barrel are not the same as the test action, chamber, and barrel, your results won't be exactly the same anyway. So load recipes are a guide, nothing more . . . and the guidance offered regarding maximum loads should be treated with respect. That said, it is also true that in today's product-liability-conscious world, most reloading manuals are very conservative. If you stay within published maximums, you probably can't get into much trouble by switching primers, playing with seating depths, and the other little tricks that can yield big payoffs in accuracy.

Choosing components is not much more complex than selecting factory loads, except that you can eventually mix and match *all* the components of the load in searching for accuracy. In most situations, you'll start by choosing the bullet you want to use. This is exactly the same as choosing a bullet in a factory load, except that your choice is wider. The good news is that the most accurate bullets—for working up loads and determining your rifle's accuracy—are generally the least expensive "over the counter" bullets, not the expensive super-premiums. Depending on the rifle and cartridge, for sheer accuracy most shooters rely on Hornady, Nosler Ballistic Tip, and Sierra. These are all very good hunting bullets as well, but for larger and/or tougher game

This is the kind of group that serious handloading can achieve. It's important to understand, however, that not all rifles—nor all barrels—are capable of such performance.

you may want to look at Speer Grand Slams, Nosler Partitions, Barnes X, Trophy Bonded Bearclaw, Swift A-Frame, Winchester Fail Safe, and such. Yes, it's confusing—but you don't have to try them all. Generally you can decide on a bullet that you like and, by changing powder charge, seating depth, etc., you can get it to shoot at least acceptably for hunting purposes.

It is far more difficult to choose the right powder, and today there are many new ones to select from. One advantage in having several reloading manuals is that you can cross-check from one to another. A powder that is listed in all the manuals for a given cartridge is probably a good bet, while a powder that is listed in only one or two may be slightly oddball for that cartridge. It could also just be a new powder that the data hasn't caught up with, so you shouldn't rule it out, but sticking with tried-and-true

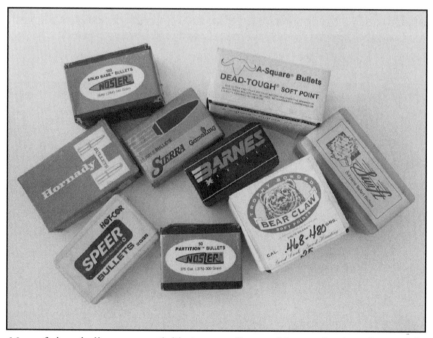

Most of these bullets are available in some flavor of factory load, at least in the common calibers. The difference is that there will be just one combination of powder and primer available. With handloads you can vary these until you find something your rifle likes.

propellants for a given cartridge is generally the best approach, especially to start with.

Some handloaders believe that simply changing the brand of primers can make a radical difference, while others pooh-pooh this idea. Like almost everything else, sometimes it matters and sometimes it doesn't—but it's always worth trying. Besides changing brands, here are a couple of other hints to keep in mind: Don't use "magnum" primers on cases of small and medium powder capacity; and if you're searching for accuracy, always try "Match" or "Benchrest" primers somewhere along the way.

Case preparation is critical not only to accuracy but also to reliability. One of the most common errors in reloading is to use too much case lubricant, which will build up in the die and dent case necks and shoulders in short order. The other most common error is failing to set the resizing die properly. Again, *read the directions.* Then read them again and make sure you understand them. On belted and rimmed cases, all you're likely to do in setting the die poorly is mess up potential accuracy (provided the round will chamber), but in rimless cases you can create an unsafe headspace problem. By the way, although neck-sized cases offer potentially the most accuracy, for hunting ammunition *always* use full-length size, and *always* use reasonably fresh cases that you have inspected thoroughly for potential cracks and separations. Personally, I don't like to go hunting with cases that have been reloaded more than once, but it's far more important to inspect them thoroughly than it is to count the number of times they have been fired.

A misfire is almost always caused by a bad primer. This is exceedingly rare in factory ammo, and it's just as rare in handloads. When it happens, it is almost invariably "operator error." Primers are relatively foolproof as they come from the manufacturer, but they can easily be contaminated by oil or spray lubricants, such as WD-40. I keep my primers stored in the original factory box, and I don't keep them very long; if I run

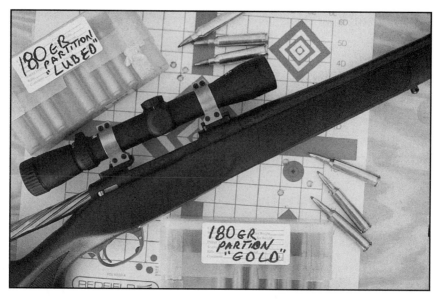

Here's a good example of a minor load variance that creates a big difference. This is a Lazzeroni 7.82 Warbird. The only difference between the bottom right group and the top left group is the former was fired with "traditional" 180-grain Nosler Partitions that have been moly-coated; the latter was fired with the new Partition Gold. All other components remain the same; there's little question which bullet this rifle likes!

across a box that's been sitting for a year or more, I will load practice ammo with those primers but not hunting ammo. Much more importantly, I never touch the primers with my grubby little fingers. I put the primers directly from the box into the hopper of a hand priming tool, swirling them around until all the bases are down, and then I seal the hopper and prime the cases. I will admit that for years I primed by hand, on the loading press—and I never, ever experienced a misfire. But I think primer seating is far more consistent by using either a hand or bench-mounted priming tool—and it's certainly better not to touch them.

As stated earlier, I weigh all of my charges. I set a volumetric powder measure a bit low, dump into the scale measure, and then bring it up to weight with a trickler . . . the same trickler I've had since I was thirteen years old. I greatly admire the electronic scales, but I don't have one. I pour charges as I always have, and I can pour about four charges per minute within $1/10$ of a grain.

I cannot tell you exactly what level of powder-charge precision is required to achieve maximum accuracy from a given load. Like everything else, it varies with the cartridge, the rifle, the load density, the powder, and so forth. There is no question that my personal desire to weigh charges to the "nth degree" of accuracy is overkill—but I feel better about my loads when I do them that way. With modern powder measures, especially when using easy-metering ball powders, I am absolutely certain that the results will not suffer in the least if I spot-check every few rounds and keep tolerances within a half-grain or so. I just prefer to do it the way I learned to more than thirty years ago.

Needless to say, a compromise is often required between accuracy and velocity; in most cases maximum accuracy with a given powder and bullet will be achieved long before maximum velocity is reached. The beauty of handloading is that you can load just a half-dozen rounds with a given charge, then go up and/ or down in half-grain increments. Your rifle will very quickly tell you what it likes and doesn't like.

For best accuracy, bullet seating depth (more properly, the distance the bearing surface of the bullet is from the lands) is often much more critical than choice of primer and the exact propellant charge (though rarely not so critical as choice of propellant). With most bullets and most rifles, the best accuracy will come from seating the bullets just a few thousandths off the lands. However, you don't want to push this too far in hunting ammo. In fact, for hunting ammo I often purposely sacrifice a bit of known accuracy in favor of a bit more velocity and/or reliability.

For instance, I might add a couple of grains of powder, knowing that I'm losing a half-inch in group size but gaining a few dozen fps. I often do this with my old .375 H&H; a tight caseful of IMR 4350 (a bit over 79 grains) is not quite as accurate as a couple of grains less of the same powder, but in my barrel the

Semi-custom ammunition is an option that's sort of in between factory ammo and handloads. I have had extremely good results with Larry Barnett's Superior Ammunition. Located in Sturgis, South Dakota (near Dakota Arms), Superior loads the Dakota proprietary cartridges, including this ammo for Dakota Model 10 in .375 Dakota Magnum.

full load yields exactly 2,600 fps with a 300-grain bullet, which adds quite a few foot-pounds over a 2,500 fps load, and makes the ballistics charts easy to use. OK, that's sacrificing accuracy for velocity, but what's this about sacrificing accuracy for reliability?

Two things to think about here. First, if your best accuracy is obtained with a bullet seated very tight on the lands, you probably want to back off a bit for field use. Especially if you're hunting under rough conditions, a bit of dirt and dust here and there can change the relationships, and you can wind up with a bullet stuck in the lands and an action full of powder. Second, when possible (especially on heavy-recoiling rifles) I prefer to use hunting bullets with cannelures, and I use the seating die (follow the directions!) to crimp the case mouth into the cannelure. Crimping is generally not the best course for optimum accuracy, and the cannelure is not likely to be located at the place that will yield the most accurate seating depth for your rifle. That's OK. Especially in situations where you may do lots of shooting, such as in Africa, I've often seen uncrimped bullets jammed down into the cases during recoil. I like to crimp when I can, even if I know I'm giving up some group size.

Well, I hope I've done my bulletmaking buddies—Randy Brooks, Bob Nosler, Chub Eastman, Lee Reid, Jack Carter, Steve Hornady—proud by presenting good reasons for handloading in today's rich factory-load environment. It isn't essential, but it is the best way to tailor ammo to your rifle and, ultimately, the best way to really get to know your rifle. We devoted an entire chapter to selecting factory loads, plus this one on handloading. I would be remiss, however, if I didn't mention yet a third course of action that sort of splits the difference. In addition to major manufacturers, there are quite a few custom and semi-custom loaders around the country. This can work in one of two ways: You can specify a load (or take a chance on the loader's recipe), or, in some cases, you can actually ship off your rifle and they will cook up a load that is actually tailored to your gun. Both methods cost a bit more than buying factory ammo and lack the personal satisfaction of working up a load yourself. But both work.

In the former instance, my primary experience has been with Larry Barnett of Superior Ammo in Sturgis, South Dakota. On several occasions I've called Larry when I had a test gun that (OK, I'll admit it!) I was just too lazy to work up a load for— and he has never let me down. He customarily loads the ammo for Dakota Arms's proprietary cartridges, and he loaded up some wonderfully accurate .30-378 ammo for me—also a very good batch of .350 Rigby Rimless Magnum. You can give Larry a specific load recipe, including your choice of bullet, and so long as it's safe he'll load it to your specs—quickly and for very little premium over standard factory ammo. Or you can trust his judgment. Either way, it's very good stuff.

My only experience with the other option, which is *true* custom reloading, is through Sam Sanjabi's "Trophy Ammo" in Chico, California. Sam basically issued a challenge: Send me a "problem rifle," and I'll make it shoot. I sent him my beat-up old .375, which has always shot 300-grain Sierra Boattails very well . . . but not much else. I asked him to work up a load that would enable me to shoot Swift A-Frames. In three weeks I had the rifle back with 100 rounds of Swift A-Frame loads and a test target showing the tightest group this rifle has shot in the fifteen years I've owned it! Sam starts with a thorough cleaning and defouling, which is often the problem; then he plays with the bedding just like we did in chapter thirteen. This is a lot of work, and it isn't inexpensive—but if you want custom-tailored ammo and haven't the time or inclination to do it yourself, I highly recommend either of these "custom ammo" routes.

Or you can just stick with factory ammo. Much of it depends on how picky you are, and how much time you're willing to spend on the range to obtain the level of accuracy and performance that you seek. No matter how it is done, finding the perfect load is rarely simple . . . but having confidence in your ammunition is, ultimately, every bit as important as having confidence in your rifle.

═══ CHAPTER SEVENTEEN ═══

SIGHTING IN

Load testing and development are all about accuracy. Exactly where the bullets land on the target makes little difference, so long as they land close together. When you sight in your rifle in preparation for hunting, this changes. Theoretical accuracy and tiny groups aren't important anymore; what matters is where the first shot from a cold barrel lands. Now the point of impact is all-critical, for the sight in you choose not only helps (or hinders) you in placing that all-important first shot but can also maximize the trajectory of your rifle.

Let's first try to understand what sighting in attempts to accomplish. It is a very simple chore, really, but fairly difficult to fully visualize—and very difficult to illustrate, because the angles involved are so slight that they defy capturing in diagrams. For instance, the typical "trajectory diagram" will show a parallel line of sight and line of bore, but a trajectory curve that rises above the line of sight, then curves back down. We've all seen such charts, and they're confusing, but, at least so far, they're about the best representation we non-technical gunwriters can come up with. Rather than show a diagram that continues the confusion, let's try it this way:

The line of sight runs exactly straight from your eye, through the scope or aligned iron sights, to the target, and on beyond to the horizon. The line of the bore, or *axis* of the bore, is also a

Use a target that will offer a good aiming point. It's okay to start at 100 yards if you're able to bore-sight or collimate, but if you aren't very sure you'll be on paper, start out much closer and avoid frustration!

straight line that runs through the center of the bore and on out to the horizon (and also rearward to the butt, determining "drop at heel and comb" stock dimensions). Depending on whether you're using iron sights or a scope (and depending on the height of your scope mounts), the line of sight is from about $^1/_2$ to $1^1/_2$ inches above the axis of the bore *at the rifle.*

Now, here's the tricky part that drawings have trouble depicting. Gravity starts affecting the bullet as soon as it leaves the muzzle. If the line of sight and axis of bore were exactly parallel, then the closest the bullet would ever be to the line of sight is that initial $^1/_2$ to $1^1/_2$-inch difference between the muzzle and the line of sight. The bullet *does not* initially rise when it leaves the bore; it immediately starts to fall, and the only *real* trajectory curve shows an ever-steepening decline from the axis of bore, starting at the muzzle. So when we sight in a rifle, we attempt to cheat the trajectory curve. The angle is far too slight to show properly on a diagram, but we actually create a very slight angle of convergence between the line of sight and axis of bore.

By doing so, we "elevate" the trajectory curve so that it intersects the line of sight. Typically, this actually occurs twice— at fairly close range, while the trajectory curve is ascending, and at longer range, after the height of trajectory is passed and the bullet is descending. What we actually do in sighting in is establish the degree of convergence between line of sight and axis of bore. The trajectory curve of a given load never changes—but by altering exactly where that bullet crosses the line of sight (both near and far) we can dramatically affect the way we *use* that trajectory curve.

For instance, let's stick with our good old .30-06, and let's use a very aerodynamic load like, say, Federal's Premium 180-grain load with a Sierra Boattail. And now I'm going to quote from one of the most valuable resources I know: Bill Matthews's *Shoot Better*. This paperbound book is 521 pages of ballistics charts covering virtually every factory load known to man, with not only ballistics data but also sight in and trajectory information. I simply can't tell you how often I use Bill Matthews's book. So let's take a quick look at what his tables (or a good computer program, or similar tables) can tell us.

Sit down at the bench and adjust your sights on a 100-yard target until your bullet lands one inch above your point of aim. It should be obvious that the bullet has already crossed your line of sight *once*, right? This happened at 37 yards. The curve of this particular load is such that one inch is pretty much the maximum height of the trajectory *with this zero*, and the bullet crosses the line of sight a second time at 158 yards.

Once the bullet crosses the line of sight the second time, its decline is accelerating, and all it can do is continue to drop faster and faster. We'd like to be able to shoot a bit farther than, say, 180 yards without holdover, so what we're going to do is increase the convergence between line of sight and axis of bore, making the bullet cross our line of sight a bit sooner the first time, strike a bit higher at 100 yards, and cross the second time at a greater range. So let's adjust our scope so that the point of impact is three inches high at 100 yards.

This small matter of two inches' difference at 100 yards changes things a great deal. The bullet crosses line of sight the first time at about 22 yards and the second time at nearly 250 yards. The height of the trajectory curve hasn't quite been reached at 100 yards—that comes a bit farther out, at 140 yards, with the bullet striking some 3.6 inches above the line of sight. The trajectory curve is exactly the same, but you've changed the way you're using it. And provided you aren't trying to hit an object smaller than 7.2 inches from top to bottom, you can now use a "dead-on" hold not only to 250 yards but even a bit farther— probably to 300 yards on a deer-size target.

At least subconsciously, virtually all of us maximize our trajectories in some fashion when we sight in. There are three primary schools of thought, and none is incorrect. I'll call them "known distance high at 100 yards," "dead-on at a given range," and "maximum point-blank range (PBR)."

The first means that you adjust your sights so that your bullet is some given distance high at 100 yards—say 2, 2½, or 3 inches. Depending on the cartridge and bullet, you know that your rifle will then be "dead-on" somewhere between about 200 and 260 yards, and you probably don't need to worry too much about holdover until the range increases to 300 yards or so.

The second means that you sight in so that your rifle is "dead on"—meaning the line of sight and the trajectory curve intersect for the second and final time—at a known point, usually a "round figure" like 200 or 250 yards. This has the same effect as the first method, but now you know exactly where your rifle is *really* "dead on."

The third, the "maximum PBR," is popular with the most studious among us. Instead of choosing an arbitrary height at 100 yards, or an equally arbitrary zero range, you let ballistics charts and computers choose the ideal zero for your range. Let's say you are going deer hunting. An average-size deer has a vital zone of at least ten inches. Let's be safe and keep our bullets within an eight-inch window (Bill Matthews calls it a "pipe," which is a good visual analogy). This means that so long as our bullet doesn't rise four inches above, or fall more than four inches below, the line of sight, we can aim "dead on" and achieve a vital-zone hit. Using the same 180-grain Federal Premium load, Matthews's book gives us the following data for an 8-inch window (4 inches maximum trajectory above line of sight): Sight in 3.5 inches high at 100 yards. The height of trajectory is 144 yards, and the bullet crosses line of sight for the second (and last) time at 259 yards. The bullet drops 4 inches below the line of sight at 305 yards, which is a very long point-blank range for a 180-grain .30-06 load.

All of these sight ins work well . . . and none of them is perfect. The great Jack O'Connor, more of a field shot than a technician, always said, "Sight in 3 inches high at 100 yards and forget about it." He wasn't too far wrong; very few loads shoot so flat that 3 inches high at 100 yards will exceed 4 inches maximum height, and with his beloved 130-grain .270 Winchester load he was very close to achieving the maximum PBR of 327 yards for an 8-inch window. I use this method a

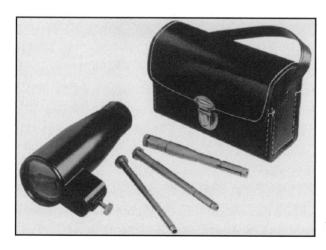

A collimator is an excellent tool for "getting on paper"— but never consider that a rifle that is only collimated is even remotely close to being sighted in. Usually collimation comes close . . . but sometimes point of impact is very, very far from where you want it.

lot—but I almost never sight in as much as 3 inches high at 100 yards. This is because I know that my most common aiming error on game is to shoot too high. I don't want an 8-inch window for myself; I don't want my bullet rising much more than 3 inches above the line of sight, and I'll gladly figure out the holdover at 300 yards to avoid shooting over the top of game at 200 yards. So I tend to sight in from 2 to 2½ inches high at 100 yards. Regardless of the sight-in height you choose, you can simply check a ballistics chart and you'll know exactly where your bullet crosses line of sight a second time, right? *Wrong!*

If you have access to good range facilities with targets set at longer distances, actually sighting in at longer range has great advantages. Unfortunately 200 yards is a bit close for a "zero range" with a flat-shooting cartridge, and 250-yard target frames are pretty scarce. If available, however, a 250-yard target would be an ideal sight-in. Of course, if you don't have access to a longer sight-in range, you can just check a ballistics chart and get the 100-yard height for a 250-yard zero and sight in accordingly at 100 yards, right? *Wrong!*

With the "maximum PBR" method you can determine your own "window." Most people seem comfortable with an eight-inch window, but I've seen so many high misses (and done them myself) with this kind of sight in that I'm much more comfortable with a six-inch window. In any case, you determine the size of the pipe. One difficulty with this methodology is that it calls for a very specific 100-yard sight in, such as "2 $^7/_{10}$ inches high at 100 yards." Few of us have rifles accurate enough (or enough shooting skill) to actually zero to the nearest tenth of an inch. But if we could, then our PBR tables would be accurate, right? *Wrong!*

The thing to always keep in mind is that regardless of the methodology you choose, any and all published data is *purely theoretical*. The only data that is real is that which you have obtained by actually shooting at known distances—and even this data is perfect only if you can absolutely duplicate the conditions. Mind you, published data is very good and will come pretty

Every time I sight in for long range I get in trouble. The David Miller Marksman was sighted dead-on at 300 yards, making it more than four inches high at 200 yards. Shooting downhill at about 375 yards, I shot over this Coues whitetail twice before connecting—and when I hit him I was aiming at his knees!

close—but never bet your life (or an important game animal) on it. There are simply too many variables, and no published data can take them into account.

For example, as wonderful as Bill Matthews's tables are, they assume that the line of sight is one and a half inches above the axis of bore at the muzzle. This is a good average, but if you have a low-power scope set in very low rings, your own height may be just one inch. If you have a big scope with a large-objective lens and high scope rings, your height could be two inches. This difference can throw off the data quite a bit—not in terms of trajectory curve but in terms of height above line of sight at various ranges.

All ballistics tables must make an assumption about height of the sight. This is not the only assumption they make. Standard published factory velocities are fairly accurate—but far from perfect. Your barrel may be shorter, longer, tighter, or looser than the factory's test barrel. If your actual velocity is within 100 fps of the published figure, that's pretty darn close. Reloading manuals, too, give velocities obtained by the load recipes *in their test barrels.* Again, your actual velocity could vary significantly.

Working with a chronograph and one of several computer programs, you *can* obtain very accurate charts for your rifle and your load. You will feed in not only the bullet weight and velocity but also the bullet's ballistic coefficient, the height of your sight, the temperature and humidity, and the elevation above sea level. If you have all of these things, then you can trust a ballistics chart. Otherwise it's just a guideline, or a good means of comparing one cartridge or load to another.

Ultimately you must choose the sight-in methodology that gives you the most confidence. I'm very comfortable with a sight in of as close to $2^{1}/_{2}$ inches high at 100 yards as I can get. Optimally, I'll also group the rifle at 200 or 250 yards, but even without more perfect knowledge, I know I don't have to worry

Once you're all sighted in, let the barrel cool and then fire a couple of shots from the kind of position you like in the field. Especially if you use bipods or tight slings, check your zero with these devices. Depending on how the barrel is bedded, some rifles shift significantly with different tension on the fore-end.

about holdover until I get beyond 250 yards. I also know that if the shot is an honest 300 yards—which is about as far as I would normally consider shooting—then I should hold high on the shoulder or just under the backbone, the difference depending on whether the cartridge is something really flat-shooting like a .300 magnum, or a more moderate cartridge like a .30-06.

I rarely get more technical than this in my approach. I quite agree that a rifle you're setting up for serious long-range work should be sighted somewhat higher, and certainly with more scientific methodology. But we agreed that this book is not about long-range work—and every time I've tried to get fancy and really maximize a rifle's trajectory, I've ended up overshooting game at moderate ranges. So the sight in I've described works for me. It's up to you to decide what works best for you.

Whatever you choose, the actual shooting techniques are pretty simple. You do want to use as steady a rest as possible so that you can eliminate human error and let the rifle shoot as well as it possibly can. In this regard, sighting in is just like test-firing for groups.

However, before we proceed to final sighting in, you must first get "on paper." The first step is to mount the scope as parallel to the line of bore as possible—but this can be very difficult to determine "by eye." Remember this, if you remember nothing else in this entire book: The only way to ensure a rifle is sighted in is to shoot it yourself until you are satisfied. That said, there are three ways to get your scope and sights in rough alignment: use a collimator, bore-sight, and shoot at very close range until the sights are close enough to be "on paper" at 100 yards. A collimator is an optical device with a "spud" that fits the bore and a grid that aligns with the scope; you bring the scope to center and you should be just fine. Sort of. The degree of accuracy varies with height of scope, so a collimator should be considered a guide only—it cannot take the place of sighting in.

A collimator is the best means of obtaining very rough zero, especially with lever-actions, semiautos, and slide-actions that preclude looking down the barrel from the breech. If you can remove the bolt (or, on a single-shot, open the action) and look down the barrel, then bore-sighting is an acceptable alternative. This is what I usually do, and I've gotten pretty good at it. You put the rifle in a solid rest and align the barrel at a target. A round bull's-eye target works best. Then, with the barrel held in place, you adjust the sights until they are also aligned with the target. It's an inexact science, and unless you're very adept at it, it's best to start at close range!

Lacking a collimator or having an action that precludes looking down the barrel, the only thing you can do is center the sights or scope on the barrel as best you can and start shooting. You can be off by an extremely large amount, so to avoid frustration and save ammo I recommend starting with a very large target at close range—no more than twenty-five yards. Once you're "on paper" at close range, move on out to at least 100 yards for final sight in.

Once you're on paper, sighting in is a relatively simple matter of adjusting your scope or sights until the bullet lands where you want it to. Here are a couple of other things to keep in mind. I do not trust "close-range" sight ins. Minor windage and elevation variances may not show up at close range, and even with good tables the proper sight in for close range depends heavily on height of scope or sights above line of bore. I also do not trust scope adjustments. European scopes tend to be pretty good in this department, but most American scopes—even good ones—are terrible. The scope may say "one click equals $1/4$ inch at 100 yards," but this is rarely precise. Worse, one click may move the impact an inch, the next a quarter-inch, the next nothing at all, and so forth. It is also not uncommon for an adjustment to not "take" until after the jarring of another shot. Unless you know your scope very well, be conservative in your adjustments, and always fire *two* shots, not just one, before making an additional correction.

The rifle should be configured just the way it will be when you take it hunting. If you plan on using a Harris bipod, it should be attached. If you plan on using a rifle sling, it should be attached. Sometimes these things make a difference in point of impact and sometimes not—but don't leave it to chance. Once you're happy with your sight in over a steady benchrest, make sure you take a couple of shots with the rifle rested on the bipod, or with a tight sling, or whatever other field shooting position you're most likely to use. Some rifles, especially those that are fully bedded or pressure-bedded, will shoot differently with the pressure of a tight sling or off a bipod than if the fore-end is rested over sandbags. Radical differences are rare, but they can occur.

Finish sighting in with the barrel in the same condition it will be when you go hunting. This means a completely cold barrel. *Do not* make your final sight adjustments with a hot barrel and

The right sight-in for you is what you're most comfortable with. What's really important isn't exactly where the rifle is sighted, but that you know exactly what it is and how that affects your trajectory curve.

think that you're done. Walk away for twenty minutes or so, then fire one last shot to be absolutely sure. If you're going to clean the rifle barrel before you go hunting, now is a good time—but do it on the range, and after you're finished fire a fouling shot. Most rifles will have a different point of impact with a perfectly clean barrel. After one or two fouling shots, most barrels will settle down to the point of impact the rifle has been zeroed to—and will stay there until barrel heat or fouling buildup causes shifting. After you've cleaned the rifle and fired your fouling shots, you'll probably want to wait until the barrel cools once more and then double-check your zero one last time. If it checks out—and it probably will—you're ready to go hunting, provided you aren't traveling great distances or changing climate dramatically.

If you've traveled to hunt, then you should always check the rifle's zero when you arrive at your destination. Mind you, there is nothing inherently insidious about air, road, or rail travel that affects rifle barrels or barrel-sight relationships. It's just that the bouncing around can cause shifting, and you must make sure everything stayed tight. Radical humidity changes make at least a theoretical difference, and changes in elevation, if radical, make a radical difference. You won't see it if you go a few thousand feet up a mountain—but if you sight in at sea level and go hunting at 12,000 feet, you can expect a significantly higher point of impact. Just check it out when you arrive—and *believe your rifle*. If there's a problem, it will tell you!

═══ CHAPTER EIGHTEEN ═══

PREPARING FOR THE FIELD

As mentioned much earlier, the day before opening day is *not* the time to start deciding exactly what load you're going to use and making certain you have enough ammo on hand. In fact, there is very little that should be left until the last minute. But let's say that you've used the summer doldrums effectively and you know what factory load or handload groups best in your rifle. If you're going pronghorn hunting, you may have decided on this most accurate load. If you're going elk or bear hunting, you may well have decided on a slightly less accurate load that offers the bullet performance you have in mind. Whatever. By now you should know how your rifle performs with the load you've chosen.

If this load differs from the practice ammo you've been using, you may need to run out to the range and make some last-minute zeroing adjustments. While you're there, this is a perfect time to run *each and every cartridge you're taking hunting* from the magazine into the chamber. Make sure each round feeds, extracts, and ejects—and catch the cartridges carefully as they eject so you run no risk of denting the cases while you're making sure they work! This procedure offers the dual benefit of function-checking both rifle and ammo. If you're on the eve of a hunting trip and you just discover that your ejector spring is broken, you didn't use your summer very well . . . but in both handloads and factory ammo (more commonly the former) you will occasionally encounter a dented case or crooked neck that won't function. Or you might have done something really stupid—like I've done on several occasions—and crafted perfectly wonderful handloads that are just a bit too long for your rifle's magazine. This is your last chance to make sure you've got it right.

If you've cleaned your rifle, this is the time to fire a couple of fouling shots and check the zero one more time. Make sure, once again, that all the screws are tight. This is your last chance. After you walk away from the range this one last time, you simply must not change *anything* without checking the zero yet again. By the way, while we mostly concern ourselves with getting the scope in zero, if there is even the remotest intent to use the iron sights as a backup, they should be checked as well. As was discussed in an earlier chapter, iron sights are not necessarily more rugged than a scope, and you should not assume that they're constantly in readiness. As was also mentioned, I don't believe in constant attaching and reattaching of even the most detachable of scopes. But if you expect your iron sights to be anything more than ornamentation, part of your final pre-hunt sight-in should include removal of the scope, checking the iron sights, reattachment of the scope, and final checking of the zero. I have been very impressed by some of the new detachable mounts—but I'd just as soon not trust them unless absolutely necessary.

I like to keep things fairly simple, and thus am not much in favor of festooning a rifle with all kinds of gadgetry. I do believe in detachable sling swivels, but highly recommend those that lock in place. If a sling swivel can become undone, it will—and if a sling or sling swivel lets go, odds are very good that the rifle or scope will sustain serious damage.

If you have sling swivels, you'll need a sling to go with them. I like a sling to be dual-purpose, used for carrying a rifle over the shoulder when you want your hands free, and to wrap your arm into as a shooting support. I don't know of any slings that are ideal for both purposes, but most will work OK both for carrying and for a "hasty sling." One type that will *not* is the padded leather

I don't like to put a lot of junk on a rifle, but a good sling is essential for most hunting situations. I tend to shoot with a tight sling, so I prefer either the old two-claw military sling or, at a minimum, a carrying strap thin enough to twist into a hasty sling.

"cobra" type of sling. They're great for carrying the rifle, but the ones I've seen are far too stiff to twist properly when you try to wrap your arm into the sling. Just as good (maybe better) for comfortable carrying are the neoprene "stretch" slings. Butler Creek offers a line of these. They will work as a hasty sling in a pinch, but the very "give" that makes them so comfortable for carrying makes them less than ideal as a shooting support.

Of course, at the opposite end of the spectrum is the good old two-claw military sling, which can be used as a true target tight sling as well as a hasty sling. I have a couple of good old leather military slings, and I use them—but the smooth leather tends to slip off the shoulder when you sling rifles with them, and they certainly aren't as comfortable as the new neoprene.

Perhaps the best compromise is a simple sling of canvas webbing. They tend not to slip, are good and rigid for use as a hasty sling, and last forever. Unfortunately I've never seen one for sale in this country that was "just right," although I've bought good ones in both Europe and South Africa. These, regrettably, are finally worn out—so now I'm on the lookout again, and I'm in hopes that some American maker will figure out how ideal a good canvas web sling really is.

I'm pretty finicky about slings because I use them all the time. I am much less finicky about scope covers—but it's a long-standing observation that you probably won't need a scope cover unless you forget to bring one. The type you choose should probably depend on what you're personally the most comfortable with. The flip-up kind, another Butler Creek/Michaels of Oregon specialty, works very well—but I've never gotten used to them and probably won't. My favorite, to tell the truth, is a thick "rubber band" cut from a section of old inner tube. With a bit of practice, you can shed it like, well, like a rubber band—and you can carve off a strip and use it for a sure-thing firestarter if you need to. But whether it's store-bought or makeshift, you should include some kind of weatherproof scope cover as part of your kit. Nothing puts a scoped rifle out of action as fast as driven rain or snow on the lens.

While we're on the subject of weatherproofing, there is very little you can do to keep a wooden stock from taking in moisture if you get caught in a protracted downpour. On the other hand, it's pretty easy to proof a stock against a bit of rain of snow. Just pull the action out of the stock—*before* you do your final sight-in shooting, *not after!*—and put a very thin layer of lacquer or other sealer on all the unfinished surfaces. I wouldn't worry too much about exterior wood finishes. The urethane finishes used by most major manufacturers will protect wood extremely well unless they're scratched through, and then they are the very devil to repair. A good old oil finish, much more attractive to my eye, probably doesn't protect the wood quite as well—but is very easy to touch

The weather you anticipate should be taken into account when prepping for a hunt. If there's any chance for rain or snow, you'll want good scope covers and some electrician's tape to put over the muzzle. If extreme weather is possible and you have a wooden stock, give serious thought to sealing the bedding.

up with a bit of linseed oil or stock compounds like Tru-Oil and the British "Red Oil."

You needn't worry about waterproofing a synthetic stock at all—but if you're anticipating some wet weather, you should apply a very light coat of a good rust preventive, like a silicone spray or Birchwood Casey's Gun Sheath, to all the steel parts of a rifle *except* the interior of the barrel. Yes, the bore can rust— but if you leave lubricant in the bore, you probably won't have the same point of impact as you will with a dry bore. The best thing to do is tape the muzzle with a strip of electrician's tape to keep out moisture and debris, and not worry about it. The tape will not change your point of impact, and it won't cause any additional pressure or anything else—all it will do is keep the bore clean and dry.

You may run into situations on lengthy hunts where you simply must clean the bore. No problem. You should definitely have cleaning gear with you, and you can clean your rifle without

Make certain you run each and every cartridge you plan on taking through the magazine and into the chamber . . . and do at least some of your final practice shooting or zeroing with a full magazine.

fear that this will cause you to miss your buck. But use plenty of clean, dry patches to get as much solvent and lubricant out of the barrel as you possibly can. The more you leave in, the greater the chance that your first shot will fly wild.

Both of these Remington .30-06 rifles that we've been playing with have turned out to be very dependable hunting rifles. The synthetic-stocked rifle, as we've seen, shot just wonderfully right out of the box. The wooden-stocked rifle turned out to be a lot less "used" than it appeared, and with just a bit of work it turned into a fine shooter as well. Neither is particularly finicky, though both like some loads and dislike others. Right now both are sighted in with good, versatile loads, and since the synthetic-stocked 700 wears a Leupold detachable scope mount, I checked the iron sights "just in case." Both rifles are absolutely ready for anything a .30-06 is capable of—which is a very broad spectrum indeed.

There is absolutely nothing special or fancy about either rifle, or about the caliber, or about their scopes or mounts. You may decide on a fancier rifle, or you may find one that is plainer. You may choose a better scope, or a scope that is more or less powerful. You may choose a good old .30-06, or you may want something more powerful and flatter-shooting—or less powerful and easier to shoot. Our .30-06s are perhaps the most versatile of North American hunting rifles—but you may decide on a much more specialized rig for your hunting. There are lots of choices out there, and it's pretty hard to make a serious mistake. Our purpose here has not been to convince you that a bolt-action .30-06 is the best choice you can make.

Whatever choice you make, you can't really be wrong so long as you come to it logically with your needs in mind. Far more important than choice of action or caliber are the steps that follow in choosing the sights, mounts, ammunition, and sight in that will enable you to get the best performance out of your rifle. We were pretty fortunate in the way our two Model 700s responded, but I wasn't particularly surprised. We had a wide assortment of ammo to try, plus the standard assortment of accurizing tricks—and we weren't looking for miracles. You may not be quite as fortunate when you start to set up your own hunting rifle—but I'll bet you will be. Provided you start with a good rifle and scope, sound mounts and good assembly, and an assortment of decent ammo—and you keep your expectations realistic—you and your rifle will do just fine. While you're figuring out what your rifle likes best, you'll get to know it very well. Whether the rifle is new or used, plain or fancy, custom or factory, what ultimately matters the most is that you have confidence in it . . . and that can only come with plenty of range time and an intimate knowledge of its likes and dislikes and idiosyncrasies. That's what setting up a rifle is all about. When you're all finished, it isn't just a rifle. It's a hunting rifle.

INDEX